MORE PRAISE FOR
PURPOSE-FILLED PRESENTATIONS

"Tony Jeary is a man with a deep well of skills and abilities found only in those few who have persevered to achieve great success."
—Dr. Robert Schuller, "The Hour of Power," Crystal Cathedral

"Tony Jeary has devoted a lifetime to learning the skills of communication and teaching them to others. I highly recommend Tony and this powerful resource to anyone desiring to go the next level in public speaking and making presentations that change hearts and minds."
—Jimmy Evans, president and founder of MarriageToday

"Tony is a man committed to helping others. His new work is sure to be a strong asset to any Christian presenting a message of any kind."
—Pastor Robert Morris, author of The Blessed Life

"I speak for a living and found Purpose-Filled Presentations to be full of valuable and applicable insights. This powerful book will help build speaking confidence to an all-time high!"
—Pat Williams, senior vice president of the Orlando Magic; author of What Are You Living For?

"This book is a great ministry tool. All you need to learn is one 7-step process to be effective to teach your Sunday school class, lead your small group, share your testimony, or train others. Tony then gives you specific examples of how to use it in those situations and more!"
—Wendy Seidman, executive director of content development & training, Willow Creek Community Church

"It has been shown that a top fear of Americans is public speaking. Purpose-Filled Presentations is filled with useful advice that will take the fear out of public speaking and help you present, witness, and communicate with amazing clarity."
—Dave Stone, senior minister of Southeast Christian Church, Louisville

"Tony Jeary is the master presenter. He writes from his wealth of experience in such a way that every teacher/speaker in any church setting can enhance their abilities to communicate effectively. His practical and simple plan will enrich anyone who desires to become a better communicator."
—Jimmy Draper, president emeritus of LifeWay

"Tony shows us that presenting is not just about being on stage; it is about communicating our ideas in ways that inspire."
—Denis Waitley, productivity consultant; author of Seeds of Greatness

"If you want to really connect with the people in your church, read *Purpose-Filled Presentations*. Whether you're a Sunday school teacher, a small group leader, or a pastor, this book will give you the tools you need to make your presentations count!"
—KEN BLANCHARD, COAUTHOR OF *THE ONE MINUTE MANAGER®* AND *LEAD LIKE JESUS*

"Tony Jeary has scored a direct hit on one of the biggest challenges facing the church today: equipping everyday members with confidence, competency, and clarity to communicate the gospel."
—DR. JIM OZIER, NEW CHURCH DEVELOPMENT OFFICER FOR THE UNITED METHODIST CHURCH

"If you are looking for a resource that will help ease the fear of presenting and impact outcomes, then utilize this work. Any Christian can win from reading *Purpose-Filled Presentations*—it's a fantastic and simple tool for any pastor or educational director to use to increase the productivity of their team."
—DR. ROBERT ROHM, AUTHOR OF *PRESENTING WITH STYLE*

"*Purpose-Filled Presentations* is essential reading for pastors, ministers, and Bible study teachers. Whether public speaking is your vocation, your hobby, or your biggest fear, this is the book for you."
—REVEREND THOMAS HARRISON, THE SECRET CHURCH SHOPPER

"First Peter 3:15 instructs us to be ready to share the reasons for the hope we have in Christ. This book offers deep insight into the process of being ready to present that hope in all its texture to anyone and everyone."
—LAMAR SMITH, AUTHOR OF *THERE'S MORE TO LIFE THAN THE CORNER OFFICE*

"This is an outstanding guide for giving great presentations. It shows you how to inspire and excite an audience on any subject."
—BRIAN TRACY, AUTHOR OF *REINVENTION*

"In today's world not only do we need to be prepared but we need to be relevant. Tony makes that easy."
—BEVERLY SALLEE, PREMIERE TRAINING CONCEPTS, LLC.

"A tremendous help for any communicator. I highly recommend this book to anyone who desires to communicate more effectively with their church, small group, or Bible study."
—DENNIS R. CULBRETH, SENIOR ASSISTANT TO THE PRESIDENT OF NORTH AMERICAN MISSION BOARD

"I have found Tony's insights into inspiring audiences to be both practical and helpful."
—JAMES O'CONNOR, PRESIDENT OF FORD MOTOR COMPANY

"Everyone who takes on the sacred moniker *Christian* wants to effectively communicate the love and joy and peace that only Christ can bring to the human heart. The problem is that most of us are ill equipped to deliver the message with power and passion. *Purpose-Filled Presentations* teaches us how to do just that."

—HANK HANEGRAAFF, PRESIDENT OF CHRISTIAN RESEARCH INSTITUTE;
HOST OF *BIBLE ANSWER MAN*

"Sharing the Gospel through effective communication is central to all who want to share their faith. Tony Jeary has transformed his proven communication techniques for use by each member of the church. This book is a must have for every ministry library."

—W.P. "BUZ" BARLOW, JR., FORMER SPECIAL COUNSEL OF WORLD VISION

"Tony clearly presents seven steps that can help any pastor, staff member, or layman improve both formal and informal communication, anywhere, any time. Once again Tony's practical, simple approach brings insights to inform, educate, and equip!"

—DAVIS H. TAYLOR, TAI INCORPORATED

"I am excited about Tony's book as it gives practical application to becoming a more effective mouthpiece for God. The real life examples and tools will quickly get you started on becoming more comfortable in any situation when discussing an aspect of your Christian walk or topics in the Bible!"

—CHRIS TUTTLE, GLOBAL NETWORK PLANNING MANAGER

"The hope-filled message of the Church is the greatest message in the world. Sharing that message and training volunteers to share it is quite another issue! Clear, compelling, and confidence-boosting, *Purpose-Filled Presentations* is packed with creative ideas. This encouraging book will make you a difference maker."

—JEFF YOUNG, MINISTER OF SPIRITUAL DEVELOPMENT OF
PRESTONWOOD BAPTIST CHURCH

"Tony's presentation ideas and best practices are a huge asset to any Christian making presentations—from small groups to Sunday morning sermons."

—STEVE DULIN, FOUNDER OF MASTERPLAN BUSINESS MINISTRIES

"Imagine giving a presentation, speech, or sermon that genuinely impacts people every time you have the opportunity. *Purpose-Filled Presentations* draws on Tony's remarkable twenty-five years of speaking experience and specifically shows how all your messages can be effective, interesting, and memorable."

—JOHN MASON, AUTHOR OF *AN ENEMY CALLED AVERAGE*

"Tony's talents have positively impacted our church and the people he's trained and coached. I so highly recommend his new book, because I know firsthand how valuable his practices can be to help any Christian present for God."

—BILL ARNOLD, OUTREACH MINISTRY OF NORTH RICHARD HILLS CHURCH OF CHRIST

PURPOSE-FILLED
PRESENTATIONS

HOW ANY **CHRISTIAN** CAN COMMUNICATE MORE EFFECTIVELY TO
ANYBODY | ANYTIME | ANYWHERE

TONY JEARY

Standard®
PUBLISHING
Bringing The Word to Life

Cincinnati, Ohio

Published by Standard Publishing, Cincinnati, Ohio

www.standardpub.com

Content development: Nonie Jobe

Editorial assistance: GoodEditors.com

Cover design: DesignWorks Group

Interior design: Dina Sorn

ISBN 978-0-7847-2314-2

Library of Congress Cataloging-in-Publication Data

Jeary, Tony, 1961-

Purpose-filled presentations : how any Christian can communicate more effectively to anybody, anytime, anywhere

   p. cm.

ISBN 978-0-7847-2314-2

1. Interpersonal communication—Religious aspects—Christianity. 2. Public speaking—Religious aspects—Christianity. 3. Pastoral theology. 4. Church work. I. Title.

BV4319.J43 2009

  254'.4—dc22   2008053409

13 12 11 10 09 08 07   9 8 7 6 5 4 3 2 1

CONTENTS

EQUIPPED WITH CONFIDENCE:

FINDING THE STRENGTH AND SKILL TO SHARE THE MESSAGE OTHERS NEED TO HEAR

> So is my word that goes out from my mouth: it will not return to me empty, but will accomplish what I desire and achieve the purpose for which I sent it.
>
> **—ISAIAH 55:11**

Everyone has a story to share. Everyone has a message to give. Whether you have been asked to teach Sunday school, lead a small group, or make a presentation in front of your church, there are people who need to hear what *you* have to say. The message, however, will not get through if you find your knees are knocking louder than you are talking. Worse yet, your lack of confidence in your speaking ability may silence your story altogether by forcing you to shirk away from the very opportunity God brings to you.

Perhaps you feel a tug to share the gospel with someone or speak up in a Bible study, but you are too intimidated by your own feelings of inadequacy. Maybe you even feel that God is calling you to prepare for full-time ministry, but you argue, like Moses did: "O Lord, I have never been eloquent, neither in the past nor since you have spoken to your servant. I am slow of speech and tongue. . . . O Lord, please send someone else to do it" (Exodus 4:10, 13).

Even if you have been involved in ministry for years, you have likely discovered that the delivery can be just as important as the message. Whether you are a novice or a veteran, you may be keenly aware you have room to grow. There is no doubt that your message is essential—you just need your audience to understand how truly important it is. If you are hungry to improve your delivery, you are in good company. Many people in the church today have incredible insight and amazing experiences, yet they just do not know how to really *reach* their audiences with the message. I offer this book to help change that.

It is tempting to think the majority of teachers and volunteers who present in the church are extroverts. The truth is, however, that many of the greatest presenters alive today are actually somewhat introverted. The ability to make a difference in another person's life through communication—and presentation—does not depend on personality type. But most effective teachers and presenters share one common trait—they have developed confidence. People who are less confident usually shy away from any type of presentation in front of a group and are sometimes even intimidated by one-on-one ministry. Ultimately, ministry involves people. Effective ministry demands that we communicate with others with confidence, conviction, and purpose. Every expert starts as a novice. In the coming pages, you will find the tools you need for confident and effective presentation, regardless of your style.

I have helped thousands of our world's CEOs, corporate leaders, and business people on all levels master the art of effective presentations, but my heart continually goes out to those in the local church who need a boost of confidence to become all God created them to be. The church is desperate for effective communication and presentation. Preaching, teaching, Bible studies, Sunday school classes, outreach ministry, missions—nearly all ministries in the church depend on one's ability to present.

You are probably aware that when people are making the critical decision about where to attend church, their choice is based on a lot more than the quality of the sermon. They consider how and if they were greeted. They carefully evaluate how the nursery volunteers connected with their children. They look to see how the Sunday school teacher relates to them and makes them feel welcome. For most visitors, the church's level of commitment to train and equip its people to communicate well through presentation translates into how much the church cares!

The church has *the* most important message, yet it may be the largest organization in the world that asks volunteers to undertake projects they have not been trained to do. Virtually no top corporation or government organization asks people to lead, organize, teach, motivate people, or plan major events without proper training. But churches do it every day. Most volunteers really want to serve. But many volunteers often do not know how to serve effectively in ministry and do not know where they can go for help. There are few resources available that teach volunteers skills—skills specific to particular ministries in the church—to help them communicate effectively through presentation.

A few years ago I coauthored a book called *Life Is a Series of Presentations*, which has as its premise the thought that many of our communication activities are actually presentations. We are presenting when on the phone with the electric company trying to straighten out a bill, when talking to our manager at work about taking some time off, or when asking someone to join our Sunday school class. With each presentation, we have an opportunity to be more effective. *Purpose-Filled Presentations* is a communication guide that will enhance ministry leaders and volunteers in delivering a variety of effective presentations within the body of Christ.

You may notice that throughout the book we use both words—*presentation* and *communication*—since one is a form of the other. Let me say here that communication is a broad term that encompasses all of the ways we interact with the world. Communication can be conveyed verbally, nonverbally, or in the written word through many types of media, including conversations, signs or billboards, books and periodicals, radio and television commercials—even a touch or a look. Although we are certainly talking about communication in this book, we are actually focusing on one form of communication: presentation.

Whether you are a church leader who wants to see your church go to the next level or a volunteer ready to move into greater ministry efficiency and influence, developing and honing your presentation skills can make a real and lasting difference in your church and ministry. Ministers and other church leaders can, by making a very minor investment, make sure their volunteers are prepared for the many presentations they must make. In fact, leaders can reenergize their churches by taking steps to make sure their volunteers are adequately trained to present effectively. This will empower volunteers to raise the bar by making very simple yet important changes in the way they present. When church leaders and volunteers learn to really reach their audiences, they enjoy ministry more, and visitors are attracted to the life and health of the church.

I have used significant research to supplement both my twenty-five-year career of helping people become better presenters and my own lifetime of experience as a volunteer at various churches. I have also gathered a special informal team of ministers and experienced volunteers in the church to help contribute to, guide, and shape this work. The end product, I believe, is a valuable resource, a unique tool, and an easy guide for the body of Christ to use to become more effective communicators in service to our Lord.

Please understand that when we are preaching, speaking, teaching, or sharing the gospel in any presentation, there is a far greater power at work than any mere human effort we may expend. We do our part when we pray and ask for the inspiration of the Holy Spirit, who is at work in both the presenting and receiving of his Word.

The book is divided into three parts. Part 1, the base, is made up of four chapters, which will teach basic communication skills that apply across the board for Christian communicators. In Chapter 1, "Communicate (with excellence)," I propose my *Seven Steps to Effective Presentations.* These steps will teach the basics of Presentation Mastery™ so your confidence will soar and you will no longer tremble when God calls you to a task that involves speaking with people. In Chapter 2, "Reduce Nervousness (and increase your confidence)," I will teach you techniques for moving "from nervous to natural," so those knees will no longer compete for your audience's attention. In the third chapter, "Prepare (to maximize effectiveness)," I will teach you how to prepare for virtually any type of presentation a Christian might be faced with, so you will know with confidence you are ready. And in the fourth chapter, "Engage (so everyone wins)," I show how to create a winning environment and connect with the person or group to whom you are speaking, whether it is from behind a pulpit, in a closed-door committee room, in a Sunday school class, in the parking lot, or on a street corner.

Part 2 of the book relates "the base" from Part 1 to specific scenarios, such as leading small groups, teaching Sunday school classes, training volunteers, leading meetings, and sharing your testimony. I apply the *Seven Steps to Effective Presentations* to each scenario to help bring clarity to your communication whys and hows. I will answer questions such as how to clarify objectives for group presentations or how to best make good first impressions.

Part 3 of the book is a list of resources that we recommend to help you further improve your skills and enhance your presentations. You will find great books listed in this section that will inspire and guide you. You'll find Web sites that will provide further information and insight on presenting in the various scenarios, as well as other tools.

Whether you are called to preach, teach, greet, encourage, or share, you will find life-changing information and techniques in this book that will help you improve what you are already doing. As you read and apply the principles and techniques in this book, you will find the confidence to respond to God's prompting and direction for the service he is preparing you to do.

PART

1

LEARNING THE BASICS

COMMUNICATE

| WITH EXCELLENCE |

> All this is from God, who reconciled us to himself through Christ and gave us the ministry of reconciliation: that God was reconciling the world to himself in Christ, not counting men's sins against them. And he has committed to us the message of reconciliation. We are therefore Christ's ambassadors as though God were making his appeal through us. We implore you on Christ's behalf: Be reconciled to God.

—2 CORINTHIANS 5:18-20

Communication is a gift from God to his people. God communicates directly to us through the Bible, and his Word is a marvelous and active presentation where he conveys his love, his ways, and his will. God empowers us to effectively reflect his image and deliver his message to the world through the gift and practice of communication. The urgency for communicating the Christian message of hope and healing to a hurting society—within the church and outside the church—has never been greater.

In today's media-driven world, the gift that God gave us to help, heal, and encourage is unfortunately often used to manipulate and distort reality in order to widen the gaps that already exist among various groups of our society. Public communication often promotes distrust, confusion, hopelessness, and intolerance rather than unity, confidence, and peace.

Our ability to communicate has a direct impact on our ability to bring God's love and hope to a searching and hurting world. First Peter 3:15 says, "Always be prepared to give an answer to everyone who asks you to give the reason for the hope that you have. But do this with gentleness and respect." Notice the communication skills mentioned in the last part of that verse and also in Colossians 4:6: "Let your conversation be always full of grace, seasoned with salt, so that you may know how to answer everyone." Gentleness, respect, and grace. We see from these verses that *how* we communicate with people can be as important as *what* we say to them! The more prepared we are with effective communication skills, the more we can answer questions with confidence, grace, and authority.

Communication has been my life's work, and I realized a long time ago that *life is a series of presentations.* God created us to live in societies and within communities, interacting daily with other people. In fact, our lives largely consist of our interactions with the people around us. Some of us may go through life without ever giving a formal speech, but very few of us go through a single day without making a presentation of some kind to someone. And if we *effectively* communicate the message of God's love to people—whether we are encouraging someone, leading a small group, sharing a thought in a class or group as a participant, or talking with a friend—we can have a profound impact on their lives.

The body of Christ is one of God's chosen vehicles for communicating the gospel. Too often, though, Christian training falls short of preparing volunteers to fulfill the charge God has given us. The *Art of Eloquence* Web site puts it like this: "It isn't enough to know God's Word; you must be able to articulate it! Understanding God's Word strengthens your faith, but being able to articulate it allows you to make a difference in the secular world and bring faith to others. You cannot effectively share or defend your faith without good communication skills. So it is equally important to know *how* to share the faith." [1]

Our churches are full of earnest followers of Christ who are called and willing to deliver God's message through the various venues of the church. But many of them lack the communication skills and confidence they need to step up to the plate. My passion is to help Christians learn effective communication tools to help them articulate the message and fulfill their calling.

While working with thousands of people over the last twenty-five years to help them become better communicators, I developed what I call the *Seven Steps to Effective Presentations.* Following these seven steps will help you make a powerful and lasting impact in whatever ministry role you serve.

I will go through the basic premises of these steps now. In Part 2 of this book, I will show you how to apply these foundational steps to specific scenarios of ministry in the church.

| STEP 1: CLARIFY OBJECTIVES |

"Before you wonder 'Am I doing things right?' ask 'Am I doing the right things?'" —Author unknown

To make your ministry really strong, I suggest you start with well thought-out objectives. Whatever your specific objectives may be for a particular area of ministry, writing them out and clarifying your purpose for each objective will set into motion a strategic thought process that will energize your efforts. Understanding the purpose—or the *why* of each objective—gives you greater confidence and increases your effectiveness. It is important that all your objectives be in alignment with the vision and goals of the church.

As you prepare your presentation, consider objectives from three different perspectives or "levels." Levels one and two relate to the overall objectives of your ministry area and are strategic in nature. Level three objectives are more tactical and specifically relate to the purpose of the presentation for which you are currently preparing.

The first level takes the broadest perspective. It is the fifty thousand-foot view where you evaluate how your presentation communicates or fits with the basic purpose of your area of ministry. This purpose will probably be established cooperatively with the church leadership or the ministry leader. Consider what you want to accomplish with this particular ministry. For example, if you are working in the first impressions ministry, your level one objective may be to create a warm and caring environment where people and relationships flourish. If you are hosting a segment of the worship service, your objective on this level may be to create a worship experience that allows people the opportunity to connect with God. A Sunday school teacher's level one objective may be to disciple people to help them grow in their faith.

The second level objectives move from a global ministry focus to a more specific but ongoing need. An objective at this level for someone ministering on the first impressions team may be to convey to guests the caring and welcoming nature of the church. For someone hosting a segment of the worship service, it may be to lead the congregation from one worship experience to another. A Sunday school teacher's level two objective may be to impart life-giving information based on a study of the Bible.

Third level objectives relate to the purpose for a specific presentation. At this level, for example, a Sunday school teacher may think about her objectives and needs for this week's Bible study. A first impressions leader may focus on a particular message the greeters need to convey to the church members for the week. And someone hosting a segment of the worship service may consider his objectives for the particular announcements he is making.

We will look more at objectives as we explore their applications in each of the scenario chapters. Clarifying your objectives will provide the important foundation for the remaining six steps in the process.

| STEP 2: DEFINE YOUR AUDIENCE |

In my book, *Inspire Any Audience*, I devote several pages in the first chapter to defining your audience. You cannot really reach an audience if you do not understand a little about who they are, what is important to them, and how they think. The more you know your audience, the more comfortable you will be during your presentation.

Form a mental image of your audience by practicing any or all of the following exercises:

- **!** Create a profile of your typical ministry audience member that includes age, background, marital status, education, income, and occupation.
- **!** If you have been an audience member in this type of group before, think through any expectations you may have had as you heard a similar presentation.
- **!** Talk with someone who has led a similar group or taught a similar class. Ask her what went well or how the experience could have been better.
- **!** If you have a list of audience members, talk to some of them in advance to see what they expect and need.

I coauthored a book with Dr. Robert Rohm that we called *Presenting with Style*. In that book, we define the DISC model of human behavior, which helps you identify and understand the different personality styles and the needs associated with each. It would help you to know, for example, that someone in your group is a High D personality type, which means he is dominant, direct, and decisive. That person would be interested in getting to the bottom line of the study or presentation quickly. A High C personality type, however, is cautious and contemplative, and she may want many more facts and details. In any group with more than three or four people, it is likely that you will have all four personality types represented, so you want to make sure there are elements of your presentation that would appeal to all. We have included a copy of the DISC model in our resource section in Part 3 of the book to enhance your understanding.

You may think you already know your ministry audience well. I believe if you follow these steps to gain a clear understanding of who your audience is, it will provide an even better foundation for the entire presentation. In *Presenting with Style* we list six subconscious needs of every member of your audience:

1. To belong
2. To be respected
3. To be liked
4. To be safe
5. To succeed
6. To be inspired

When you help meet the needs of your audience members, you create an incredible opportunity to reach them and make a real difference in their lives. Knowing your audience is crucial to knowing how to meet their needs. As you will find later in Step 7: Close with Action, it's imperative to understand the needs of your audience so you can identify the actions you want them to take to meet those needs.

Once you have clarified your objectives and defined your audience, then you are ready to start gathering the content for your presentation.

STEP 3: GATHER CONTENT

By now you have clearly defined and written down your objectives for your presentation, which will serve as the foundation for the materials you gather. In many ministry presentations, people are often tempted to develop their points and then try to find how the Bible may back those points up. Scripture is a much more effective guide if we gather what it says about the subject first and then allow God's Word to help shape our thoughts and points.

Whatever sources you use, make sure they align with your church's doctrine, goals, and vision. Above all, maintain what I call "Bible richness." In other words, keep the content of your presentation as accurate to the Bible as possible. Be careful not to put your syllabus or opinion ahead of Scripture. If you do include an opinion, be careful to label it as just that. Life questions and challenges that come up obviously need to be addressed from the biblical viewpoint, and not just from a personal opinion.

Start keeping a file to collect testimonies, stories, anecdotes, jokes, quotes, or ideas that may be pertinent to the subject matter of your ministry area. Using the information you gathered will help validate your points and will make your presentation more convincing and powerful. You can collect these items through books, magazines, and other printed resources on your topic, or you can search for them on various Web sites. There are a number of Web sites that exist to provide teachers, speakers, and researchers with illustrations and ideas on an endless variety of topics. We have listed some in Part 3.

Remember to gather any visual aids you might want to use. A complete PowerPoint presentation may be a little overwhelming for small groups, but you can spice things up with handouts.

Keep your presentation practical and realistic. Most people want practical knowledge and application rather than something abstract and unattainable. Information presented in an easy-to-remember format, like a simple acronym or a three-point message, is easier to digest and retain.

You have done your homework by defining your audience and their needs. Their needs should, in fact, be the very core of your presentation. Now that you have gathered your content, it is time to really get ready!

STEP 4: MAXIMIZE PREPARATION

My experience in launching into a new career is a perfect example of what happens if you *do not* live by the Boy Scout motto, "Be prepared." I had great success and failure in my twenties as an entrepreneur. In my late twenties, I changed careers and decided to move toward advising and encouraging others.

As I look back on my first speaking engagement some twenty-plus years ago, I remember an unprepared young man strutting to the stage with overhead transparencies. Once on the stage, I realized to my horror that I was facing almost two thousand pairs of eyes. I started to sweat. I threw my first slide up and started telling myself, *I can do this. My story is real. I have something of value to give to these people.*

As I started telling my story, people in the audience began to laugh and point. I was even more shaken when I found out why—my transparencies were upside down! I had lost my opportunity to make a good first impression, and my confidence was shattered. I remember standing alone at the front of the room, detached from my audience, and fumbling through my presentation. Then the unthinkable began to happen—people started getting up and leaving the room in the middle of my presentation!

Miraculously, my promoter did not fire me that day. We certainly went back to my hotel room for the first of many postmortem meetings, but we continued the tour he had booked for the remainder of the year. It was a learning year, and I was determined to find a way to improve my presentation effectiveness. I began reading hundreds of books and watching dozens of videos of every successful presenter I could find, hoping I could learn from the masters how to make excellent presentations. Through hard work, new insight, and God's grace, I became a master presenter myself. In his mercy and plan, God has given me the privilege of coaching many others along the same lines for a number of years now.

I have learned so much since that eventful first day. I can see now that one mistake was that I had approached my first seminar presentation with insufficient preparation. I certainly did not know the seven basic steps for effective presentation, or how to complete a 3-D Outline™ (which we will discuss later in this chapter). I had not even thought through the process of knowing my audience well and really determining their needs or getting comfortable with my venue. But what I did learn from that experience was this: *preparation pays huge dividends.* Whether you are presenting for a small group or making a presentation in front of a huge audience, preparation can mean the difference between connecting and calamity.

A special concept I teach my clients is something I call "planned spontaneity." Ideally, you should know much more about your subject than the information you include in your presentation. This does not mean you have to be a Bible scholar with fluency in Greek and Hebrew when you make a presentation to your ministry audience. It simply means that you need to be very familiar with your presentation subject. A great way to do that for a biblical theme, for example, is to use a Bible that has cross-reference Scriptures in the margin. Look up those verses and gain an understanding of their relevance to your subject. You can look up the passage you are teaching in several Bible commentaries to gain more depth on the subject. The better "information cushion" you have, the more your confidence will build and the more spontaneous you can be when someone asks a question or brings up a point outside the parameters of your presentation.

If someone happens to ask a question you were not able to cover in your "information cushion," feel free to say something like, "I don't know the answer to that. Can anyone else here help us?" That frees you from having to say something you are not sure is accurate and helps you retain your credibility.

I also like to teach my clients the concept of maximizing preparation through a process called "strategic thinking." There is an important difference between focusing on the tactical (the *hows*) and focusing on the strategic (the *whys*). Once you have defined your objectives for your ministry and are clear about the *whys* related to them, you will be able to better prepare the *hows* with clarity and focus. There are many distinctions involved in planning, and everything you do should be driven by the strategic *why*.

As you engage the strategic thinking process, make a checklist of the tactical things to be done to achieve your objectives. The checklist could include details like furnishing background music, setting up the room, obtaining a flip chart or a white board with markers and erasers, preparing the food to be served, making copies of handouts, furnishing writing pads and pencils, and asking someone to pray before or after the meeting. Strategic thinking will take you all the way through to the end of the presentation process. Through this process, you will not lose sight of the far-reaching effects and benefits of your presentation by getting lost in or overwhelmed by the short-term tactics and activities.

| THREE-DIMENSIONAL OUTLINE |

Like many of my clients, you may find that the 3-D Outline™, a presentation development instrument I designed years ago, can become your most valuable tool as you begin sorting through your material. It not only helps you to organize your thoughts and actions as they relate to your audience, objectives, key points, and timing, it also conserves your valuable time and allows you to focus on the big picture.

In essence, the 3-D Outline™ helps you look at all three dimensions of your presentation—the *what*, the *why*, and the *how*. Unfortunately, most people focus only on the *what*. If you immerse yourself in the *why* of each of the *whats*, you can further insure that each minute counts.

As you build your 3-D Outline™, you will see that it also helps you think through the timing of your presentation and prepare in a way so that the timing can be better managed. As you do this for each segment (the *what* dimension) while considering the other two dimensions (*why* and *how*), keep in mind that you want to avoid boredom and stay within the time allowed.

The 3-D Outline™ also gives you the option of adding another element— the *who*—if more than one person is involved in the presentation.

Let's review the three dimensions and the additional two elements:

❗ **What (The First Dimension):** This column identifies each segment of your presentation and is where you will record a brief description of your introduction, opening, main points, and closing. You can see a complete example on page 52 or at *www.PurposeFilledPresentations.com*.

❗ **Why (The Second Dimension):** This column is for recording why you have chosen the *what* segments you will present. It helps you keep focused on your objectives. Make sure all of your *whats* support the objectives you have chosen for your presentation.

❗ **How (The Third Dimension):** The *how* column indicates the method of delivery. Ways to communicate in a group setting include talking, flip charts, PowerPoint, stories, testimonies, role-playing, games, activities, trivia, quizzes, videos, movie clips, or audio clips. Be aware of the wide variety of delivery approaches and think through the best ways to keep excitement and inspiration in your presentation. Since the adult attention span is approximately five to seven minutes, it is usually a good idea to change delivery methods at least that often.

❗ **Time:** This column is for recording the estimated amount of time you will have to cover each of the *what* segments of your presentation.

❗ **Who:** This is a fifth column you can add if more than one person will be involved in the presentation delivery. For example, if you have arranged ahead of time for someone to tell how the information you are present-ing has affected her life, you will want to include that as a separate *what* segment and put the person's name under the *who* column.

Once you get into the 3-D Outline™, you will see that it is quite simple. A blank outline is shown below and you can download a free template at www.PurposeFilledPresentations.com. In Chapter 3 we will go into more detail on the 3-D Outline™. In most scenario chapters there will be a sample of a completed outline that pertains to that particular area of ministry. This will help you gain a more complete understanding of how to maximize this tool.

3-D OUTLINE™

Presentation Title:		Del. Date:
Audience:		Start Time:
Objectives:		End Time:

Final Preparation Checklist:	[ ]	[ ]
	[ ]	[ ]

#	Time	What	Why	How	Who
1.					
2.					
3.					
4.					
5.					
Total Time					

| STEP 5: OPEN WELL |

"You are an unknown quantity for only 120 seconds. After that, everything you say will be heard in the context of the impression from your first two minutes."—DAVID PEOPLES, *PRESENTATIONS PLUS*

People generally make a judgment about a person or a presentation within the first two to three minutes. If you do not connect with them early, you could be playing catch-up for the rest of the presentation. Here are two practices for making a good first impression that I believe apply to presentations in virtually any scenario:

1. Show respect and build rapport. These elements provide a threshold for audience buy-in, involvement, and satisfaction. The first words out of your mouth should carry your audience over this threshold and prove that you will, above all else, deliver these audience imperatives.

! Make the audience your partner. One way to guarantee an audience's commitment and loyalty to you is to immediately involve them in your presentation. The key to audience buy-in (a prerequisite for audience inspiration) is to make them part owners of the presentation. Once your audience has taken partial ownership of the presentation, you are destined for success. There are three steps to making the audience your partner:

● Meet as many attendees as possible before the presentation. This begins to build a one-on-one bond that will carry over into the first few minutes of your presentation.
● Prove you respect them by starting the presentation on time.
● Ask them to define their own expectations. This gives them input and lets them know you care about what is important to them.

! Prove you respect their time. You have put a lot of effort into preparing your presentation. Why? Because you care about your audience and respect their time. At some point in your first three minutes, let them know that because you respect their time, you have invested hours of preparation in your presentation.

! Prove you have prepared. Nothing sends the message that you don't care like being unprepared. Every detail counts. Start on time. Have the appropriate materials ready. Know what you are going to say. Audience members notice virtually everything, and if they get the feeling that you are ill prepared, they may tune you out. In order to better demonstrate readiness, make sure you are prepared with the answers to some questions that may be important to them. Such questions include:

- Who are you?
- What is the objective of your presentation? (purpose)
- What is the agenda for the presentation? (process)
- What can be gained from the presentation? (payoff)

! Empathize with your audience and communicate similar interests. Acknowledge audience members by name (by using nametags if necessary). Show some commonality; people like people who are like themselves. Let your audience know that through your preparation you have gained the same benefit they will receive from your presentation and that you are excited to share it with them.

! Use eye contact. Start your first few minutes by making solid eye contact with a few members of the audience. Do not just scan the audience—speak *to* individuals. Even those with whom you are not making eye contact will benefit because they will be able to see that you are talking to individuals. In addition to creating the impression that you are confident and honest, eye contact keeps your audience members alert and communicates your interest in them.

2. Open with a comment to grab the audience's attention and then run with it. The line does not have to be outrageous, just interesting. It should also be something that gets the audience involved at some level, even if it is only to raise their hands or answer a question. Here are some ideas to grab the audience's attention:

! Find a hook.

- Begin with a startling or interesting statistic.
- Ask a proactive question.
- Tell a story about something that recently happened to you or a story about the theme you will be presenting.
- Refer to some current newsworthy event.

! Know and use different types of openers.

● Current events. Open with a comment on some local or national event that makes a point about your subject.

● Humor. Start with a funny story, observation, or activity. Make sure it is pertinent to your topic or illustrates some point you wish the audience to understand. Remember, laughing gets the audience on your side! Unless you are really gifted in telling jokes, however, it is best to avoid them.

● Pictures. You have heard the proverb, "A picture is worth a thousand words." Showing a picture with a message can be a powerful opening.

● Anecdotes. Share an anecdote illustrating an important concept included in your presentation. The key to using anecdotes is to keep them short and to the point. It is better to tell a short story and leave the audience wanting more than to draw a story out to the point of boredom.

● Pertinent quotes. Quotations are often filled with wisdom and carry authority, and they may make a point more clearly than we can. Of course, the Bible is the best source for wise and authoritative quotes.

● Real-world situations. A recognizable scene grabs attention. Audiences respond to "seeing themselves" in a situation. Create a scene the audience can relate to and one that has a powerful impact in your presentation.

● Music. Music is effective. It can move the audience and be used to make a point. Choose music that fits your objective.

There are certain ways to *kill* an opening:

! Apologizing. Do not start your presentation with an apology like "I am not much of a speaker (or teacher or leader), but here goes." Doing so can set you up for failure. Think positively.

! Using an unrelated or inappropriate anecdote. A presentation has to be *about* something. If your stories or anecdotes are unrelated to the topic, they can confuse your audience.

! Beginning with long or slow-moving statements. Open with a bang and move on. Stay a step ahead of the audience. This does not mean talking fast; it means do not dawdle when telling stories or making points.

As we go through the various scenarios in Part 2 of the book, I will suggest ways to incorporate these best practices.

It is crucial to open well and start with a bang, but that is only the beginning.

| STEP 6: ENGAGE YOUR AUDIENCE |

The days of lectures and one-man shows are long gone. People today do not want to be "talked at." Rather, they want to have a conversation with you. Various surveys conducted over the years indicate that the average person retains about ten percent of what he reads, twenty percent of what he hears, thirty percent of what he sees, fifty percent of what he hears and sees, seventy percent of what he says, and ninety percent of what he says and does. The more you engage the members of your audience, the more "takeaways" they will have. Involving them is one of the best ways to keep their attention. Consider leading your audience about half of the time and "facilitating" the other half by guiding others to participate.

There are numerous ways to involve your audience. You can call people by name, ask them to take notes, or have them read something aloud. Use handouts, ask questions, and encourage humor. I use a lot of what I call "*Strategic Engagement*" in my presentations. One of my favorite *Strategic Engagement* methods is to pass out dollar bills in reward for audience participation. In a ministry setting, it may be fun to hand out candy, bookmarks, or other inexpensive trinkets. Find and use your own style.

If you are leading a small group, Bible study, Sunday school class, or a youth ministry, engage your audience by using open-ended questions that allow people to speak from their own perspectives. Using questions such as, "What do you think about that?" or "How does this apply to you?" will usually get people talking. You may want to address your first question to an extrovert, then call on others as the comfort level climbs. If one of your listeners has a passion about a certain subject, ask her to share her insights with the group. But be ready to politely steer her back to the agenda! If you are concerned that people will not respond to your question, have them share in pairs first to begin thinking about the question. Then ask people to share what they think.

Remember, not everyone has to be involved in a discussion. As the leader, your goal should be to make your presentation a win for everyone in the group. If someone does not want to talk, pushing that person to answer a question will most likely not produce a win for you or the group member. Once a person decides to join the discussion, simply ask her to share more to encourage involvement. Just be sensitive to know when to encourage discussion and when to move on.

Another way to create a winning scenario is to give sincere compliments and show genuine appreciation. Be generous (but heartfelt) with comments like, "Thanks for the way you answered that," or "That's really eye-opening," or even, "That's fantastic!" People will be more prone to participate in a discussion if they know their contributions are appreciated. As you create an atmosphere that encourages and promotes discussion, you will find that your audience will contribute more and work with you to apply what you are sharing. Speaking of application, let's look at the last of our seven steps.

| STEP 7: CLOSE WITH ACTION |

Toward the end of your presentation, elicit feedback from your audience to see how they are going to put your principles and objectives into action. The first step for real change is their understanding and buy-in of your presentation objectives. I like to come right out and ask people for their biggest takeaway from our time together. Challenge them to think of some action they will take. By suggesting a few action points, you can help them begin considering the possibilities.

Earlier in this chapter, I talked about the six basic subconscious needs of every member of your audience. If you allowed your audience members to list their expectations at the beginning of your presentation, they were expressing their needs. When you close, review those expectations to show them how you met or exceeded them. By doing this, you will be able to show them how you have met their needs. The call to action should bring your points and objectives together and give the group members a reason to be glad they attended.

In this chapter, I have given you the basics to the *Seven Steps to Effective Presentations*. You will find more detailed instruction tailored to various ministry scenarios in subsequent chapters. I encourage you to study these techniques, as well as those in the next three chapters. I challenge you to put forth diligent effort toward becoming the best messenger you can be. Once you have the tools in your hand, it is up to you to decide what to do with them. The more you study, apply, and practice, the more effective you will become.

| THE PRESENTATION MASTERY IMPACT CURVE |

"And whatever you do, whether in word or deed, do it all in the name of the Lord Jesus, giving thanks to God the Father through him" —COLOSSIANS 3:17.

We are reminded in Colossians 3 that everything we do should be done in the name of the Lord. I don't know about you, but if I do anything in the name of the Lord, I want to do it well. My mother always told me that anything worth doing is worth doing right. Her advice was scriptural.

I have a theory that I demonstrate through a model called the *Presentation Mastery Impact Curve*. This model gives a visual representation of a person's level of effectiveness in any particular area. It illustrates that the exponential difference between the basic and mastery levels of presentation is similar to the dramatic difference between ordinary and extraordinary performance. Individuals who work diligently to move beyond average performance typically experience results that, over time, far exceed those who choose to remain average.

When you look at the *Presentation Mastery Impact Curve* model on the next page, notice that the impact does not increase significantly until effectiveness is achieved in the mastery level. Many people have developed their presentation skills to some degree, or perhaps they were gifted with a certain amount of natural ability at birth. Maintaining that level just keeps them even with the game. Sadly, the vast majority of people are content to stay within the basic range of effectiveness and typically do not reach their full, God-given potential.

As you see in the model, early in the development of skills small advances produce proportionately small improvements. But once the basic and advanced components of a skill set (levels 1 and 2) have been mastered, incremental improvements begin to yield exponential results (level 3).

For example, you would probably agree that Michael Phelps is one of the most accomplished swimmers in the world. He was only twenty-three years old when he won eight gold medals at the 2008 Olympic games in Beijing. To have reached that level of accomplishment at such a young age, you would think he had started out swimming like a dolphin as a toddler. Both of his older sisters were talented swimmers, but he didn't start lessons until the age of seven, when his mom enrolled him to give him an outlet for his grief over his parents' divorce. But when he started the lessons, he was terrified of putting his face in the water. He hated it. According to his book *Beneath the Surface*, it was a "screaming, kicking, fit-throwing, goggle-tossing hate." [2] His instructor finally compromised and started him out swimming on his back.[3] From the age of seven until he was eleven (just four years before he became the youngest swimmer to compete for the U.S. in the Olympics in sixty-eight years), he was operating at the basic level of mastery.[4]

PRESENTATION MASTERY IMPACT CURVE

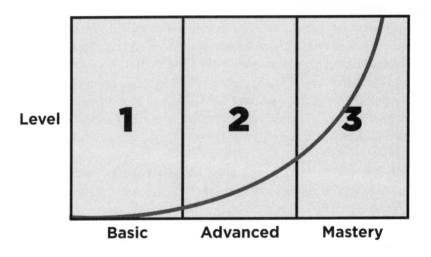

What happened between age eleven, when Michael was little more than an average athlete, and his incredible rise to becoming a globally recognized superstar? In 1996, he watched swimmers Tom Malchow and Tom Dolan compete in the summer games in Atlanta, and he began to dream of becoming a champion. He knew some things had to change for him to achieve that dream. He realized that he needed better training facilities than the local high school pool and more professional coaching. He moved to the North Baltimore Aquatic Club at the Meadowbrook Aquatic and Fitness Center, where he met Bob Bowman a year later, the man who would coach him to Olympic history. Bowman recognized Michael's potential immediately. Fiercely competitive, Michael took to Bowman's instruction well and worked hard. He started competing and winning for the aquatic club team. At that point, I think we could safely say he was operating at the advanced level.

But he did not stop there. During Michael's sophomore year in high school, his performance convinced him that he could become the champion he dreamed of being. He increased his training regimen considerably and began working out ten times a week. He watched tapes of Olympic champions like Australian Ian Thorpe, and he read books on sports heroes like Lance Armstrong and Vince Lombardi. By the time he was fourteen, Michael had earned a spot on the U.S. Nationals B Team and started breaking records. At fifteen, he ranked seventh in the world in the 200-meter butterfly and forty-fourth in the 400-meter individual medley. He continued breaking records, winning titles, and scoring victories. Never satisfied, even in victory, Michael and his coach huddled after events and picked apart his technique to determine where he could improve. Michael won six gold and two bronze medals in the 2004 Olympics. On his way to winning eight gold medals in the 2008 Olympic games in Beijing, newscasters repeatedly remarked that he had developed an uncanny ability to focus. Through this diligent effort, he not only became a superstar, but a master of his sport.

We can achieve mastery with the things God has called us to do in life. If you are serious about becoming all God wants you to become and being the most effective messenger for him you can be, I would encourage you to go the extra mile in your pursuit of presentation effectiveness.

I have invested years in the study of presentation effectiveness. And, like Michael Phelps, I have put a tremendous amount of effort into studying the masters in my field and practicing to perfect my game. *Purpose-Filled Presentations* contains many of the lessons and principles I have learned in the communication trenches during those years. I am blessed to be able to share them with you.

In the next chapter, "Reduce Nervousness (and increase your confidence)," you will learn how to overcome your presenting fears by turning many of your unknowns into knowns. I believe that if we can discover the source of our nervousness, we can conquer it. You will find proven tips for conquering your fears and gaining a confident state of mind.

CHAPTER 1 VIP'S

! Communication is a gift from God to his people. He empowers us to effectively reflect his image and deliver his message to the world through the gift and practice of communication.

! *How* we communicate with people can be as important as *what* we say to them. If we *effectively* communicate the message of God's love to them, we can have a profound impact on their lives.

! Whatever your specific objectives may be for a particular area of ministry, writing them out and clarifying your purpose for each objective will set into motion a strategic thought process that will energize your efforts. It is important that all your objectives be in alignment with the vision and goals of your church.

! You cannot really reach an audience if you do not understand a little about who they are, what is important to them, and how they think. When you help meet the needs of your audience members, you create an incredible opportunity to reach them and make a real difference in their lives.

! Whatever sources you use to gather your content, make sure they align with your church's doctrine, goals, and vision. Above all, maintain "Bible richness."

! People generally make a judgment about a person or a presentation within the first two to three minutes. If you do not connect with them early, you could be playing catch-up for the rest of the presentation.

! People today do not want to be "talked at." Rather, they want to have a conversation with you. The more you engage the members of your audience, the more "takeaways" they will have.

! Toward the end of your presentation, elicit feedback from your audience members to see how they are going to put your message into action.

1. Artofeloquence.com, http://artofeloquence.com/catalog.php?item=40&ret=articles.php (accessed August 6, 2008).

2. Michael Phelps and Brian Cazeneuve, *Beneath the Surface* (Champaign, IL: Sports Publishing L.L.C., 2004), 16.

3. Ibid., 16-17.

4. Information in this section was taken from "Michael Phelps Biography," which can be accessed at Jockbio.com, http://www.jockbio.com/Bios/Phelps/Phelps_bio.html.

REDUCE NERVOUSNESS

| AND INCREASE YOUR CONFIDENCE |

> For God has not given us a spirit of fear, but of power and of love and of a sound mind.

—2 TIMOTHY 1:7 (NKJV)

"Everyone has butterflies in their stomach. The only difference between a pro and an amateur is: the pro has the butterflies in formation!" **—ZIG ZIGLAR**

Polls have shown that Americans fear public speaking more than death. The good news is that as a Christian, you do not have to fear death *or* public speaking. God has provided a way for the former through his Son, Jesus. And he has also promised to give you everything you need to accomplish what he has called you to do when you face the latter.

For years people have conducted various surveys and published reports that indicate that about half of us are sometimes nervous when we have to speak in public, twenty-five percent of us struggle with anxiety but manage despite the stress, and another twenty-five percent are so fearful that we avoid meetings, refuse promotions, or change jobs to escape an audience! As far as I know, stage fright has never killed anyone, but it has stopped people from sharing the message God has given them to share. It has kept people from moving forward in their careers, robbed people of making valuable contributions, and hindered countless ministry opportunities.

Perhaps you've been asked to teach an adult Bible class. You feel that God has been nudging you in that direction for some time, because you really enjoy studying the Bible. You know from your experience with teaching young children that you are a competent teacher at the very least. But teaching adults, you tell yourself, is a totally different ball game. As you imagine yourself in front of the class, your hands start sweating, your knees feel weak, and your mouth goes dry. How are you ever going to be able to walk into that classroom and teach your lesson?

If I have described something similar to what you have experienced, just know that you are not alone. As I have traveled the world over to train thousands of people how to present well, I have heard story after story of the excruciating fear and outright panic people face as they endeavor to make a presentation. I have found that the most common reason people are nervous when it comes to presenting is the simple fact that they fear the *unknown*. I have also seen that once they have discovered the source of their nervousness, they have been able to conquer it. I am convinced that you will as well.

Here are some common sources of fear:

! How the audience will react (including boredom or even hostility)
! Forgetting an important detail or point
! Looking or feeling foolish
! Not living up to the audience's expectations
! Not living up to your own expectations
! Being the center of attention
! Speaking to an audience of different status (such as education, income, or race)
! Unfamiliar situations

The chart on the next page can be used as a handy reference guide to help you overcome the fears listed above. The solutions listed in the chart are discussed in greater detail in this chapter, as well as in Chapters 1, 3, and 4.

FEAR	SOLUTION
Audience reaction	Know your audience; grab their attention in the first three minutes and keep them engaged, connected, and smiling.
Forgetting an important detail	Maximize preparation; use 3-D Outline™ and checklists.
Looking foolish	Know "above and beyond" your subject; be real and share from your heart.
Not living up to audience's expectations	Survey your audience's expectations in advance—by phone, e-mail, or in person—and adjust your objectives accordingly; keep them engaged and connected during the presentation.
Not living up to your own expectations	Do not expect perfection; maximize your preparation, rehearse, and do your best.
Being the center of attention	Talk *with* your audience instead of *at* them; get them involved in activities to get their eyes off of you.
Speaking to an audience of different status	Look your best and act confident; greet audience members as they come in and spend a few minutes getting to know them and letting them get to know you. Build rapport immediately.
Unfamiliar situations	Know your room, your equipment, your props, and your presentation. Consider possible problems and prepare for them.

Keep in mind that a little nervousness before a presentation is healthy. It shows that your presentation is important to you and that you want to do well. The day I stop being nervous is the day I know I am no longer an effective presenter. You can make your nervousness work for you rather than against you by converting nervous energy into enthusiasm. Remember that no matter what ministry area you are working in—whether it is greeting, leading a Bible study, teaching a class, helping in an outreach ministry, serving on the board or on a committee, or working in a crisis pregnancy center—you are working to strengthen others in Christ, and you have something of value to give to your audience.

Your own negative thoughts may be creating additional unnecessary anxiety. Concentrating on thoughts like, "I can't possibly do a good job with this presentation," or "I don't have anything of value to contribute," undermines your confidence, interrupts your planning, and increases your fear. Negative thoughts create tension in your body, which sends distress signals back to your mind. Your mind then comes up with even more negative thoughts, and an endless cycle of anxiety begins.

Second Corinthians 10:5 tells us to take every thought captive to the obedience of Christ. Instead of concentrating on negative thoughts and worries, believe and repeat Philippians 4:13: "I can do all things through Christ who strengthens me" *(NKJV)*. Not only has God given you gifts and talents to enable you to present successfully, but he will also give you extra strength and grace when you need it!

Before I go more into proven tips to help you turn your "nervous into natural," let me stop here and acknowledge that true peace comes from God. Philippians 4:7 reminds us, "And the peace of God, which transcends all understanding, will guard your hearts and your minds in Christ Jesus." And Colossians 3:15 tells us to "Let the peace of Christ rule in your hearts." Believe God's Word, pray, and ask God to give you peace before you undertake any presentation.

It is important to remember, however, that we have a vital part to play in every presentation. If you examine the context of the verse we just looked at in Colossians, you'll find that verse twenty-three of the same chapter says "Whatever you do, work at it with all your heart, as working for the Lord, not for men." In other words, God asks us for our very best in everything we do, because we are doing it for his glory.

God does not expect perfection, and neither should we. Trying to achieve perfection is futile and leads to anxiety. But God wants and expects us to do everything we can to create an excellent presentation. After we have done all we can, we should rest in peaceful confidence that things will go well. And we need to remember that even if things do not go as planned, God will use everything in our lives for good and for his purpose.

We can experience fear when we face more unknowns than knowns. When this sort of fear stems from a lack of adequate preparation, it is justifiable. Therein lies the secret to conquering much of our nervousness. Preparation—taking the unknown and turning it into the known—builds confidence. Preparation pays huge dividends! If you are well prepared and still feel nervous (as almost everyone does), your preparation will take over once you begin your presentation, and your nervousness will begin to diminish. That is especially the case if you concentrate on the message you want to convey and, more specifically, the objectives you want to accomplish.

Using the *Seven Steps to Effective Presentations* to Conquer Your Fears

I developed the *Seven Steps to Effective Presentations* that we looked at in the first chapter to teach my clients how to plan well for their presentations and significantly reduce their fear. Now we are going to see how each step can help you reduce nervousness and increase confidence.

Step 1: Clarify Objectives

As you prepare for your presentation, your objectives should keep you grounded and focused. When you concentrate on *why* you are doing what you are doing, as opposed to just *what* you are doing, your nervousness will begin to take a backseat. As you feel fear creep in, go back to your objectives. They will remind you how important your presentation is and how your audience needs you to push through your fears.

Step 2: Define Your Audience

Take time before your presentation to find out about your audience and what their needs are. Then spend your time thinking about their needs rather than worrying about yourself. Remember that this presentation is not really about your performance. Rather, it is about the growth that occurs in your listeners. You are delivering the message, but real change will come from the Holy Spirit working in the hearts of your audience. You have something they need and are giving them a valuable gift in the message of your presentation. When your audience feels that you care about them, their warmth will melt your nervousness away.

Before your presentation, find the answers to these questions to help you work through your fears:

! Who will attend?
! What are their concerns?
! Why will they attend?
! Are they already familiar with your subject?
! What do they want or need to learn from your presentation?
! What do they know about you?
! Will you have to establish credibility with them?
! What is in your presentation for them?

When you know your audience's expectations, you become much more confident. You may need to get this information from people who know your audience members, or you could survey your audience electronically and ask them for feedback prior to your presentation. You may be able to get even more information by doing some research about this particular demographic or age group.

View your presentation as an interaction between you and your listeners—a chance for you to share ideas with each other. Remember, you want to engage your audience and talk *with* them instead of *at* them. As you prepare to do this, you will be less likely to be wrapped up in your fears.

| STEP 3: GATHER CONTENT |

Step three brings us to the number one rule in combating nervousness: Do not procrastinate! Ironically, fear of presenting often causes us to delay getting started. The less time you have to adequately prepare and rehearse, the more pressure and nervousness you feel. Don't get caught in this vicious cycle.

As you gather your materials, gather "above and beyond" the actual content of your presentation. If you are teaching a topic from the Bible, use cross-reference Scriptures, Bible dictionaries, concordances, and commentaries. If you are presenting on a family issue, find articles and books by Christian authors and read everything you can get your hands on. If you are making a presentation to your fellow board members, know as much as you possibly can about the subject. Anticipate your audience's questions and be prepared with the answers. If you are witnessing to your neighbor, memorize or highlight Scriptures that tell of the plan of salvation. It also helps to watch current events, because everything we do as Christians is affected by the world around us, and current events may pop up at very unexpected times in your presentation.

There is no way to know everything about your topic, and it is easy to get lost in a sea of research and searching. As you gather information, gauge what you can realistically learn in the time you have before your presentation. Do not allow your research and gathering to lead you toward a dead-end or tangent. If you gather a solid base of information, you can have confidence that your presentation will deliver your objectives.

| STEP 4: MAXIMIZE PREPARATION |

By the time you complete your 3-D Outline™, you should be very comfortable with the components of your presentation, as well as your visual aids.

From your outline, make a complete checklist of the things you need to do before your presentation. Make sure you include detailed items such as getting equipment, copying handouts, bringing music, and setting out pads and pencils. Be sure to put venue contact names and numbers on your checklist, if appropriate, as well as phone numbers for anyone else you may need to call. Knowing your action items are written down and close at hand will give your brain—and your nerves—a break.

If you will be using signs or flip charts, prepare as many as you can in advance so you won't be worrying about timing or misspelling. The more you can prepare in advance, the more you can focus on your audience during your presentation. Prepare one flip chart or handout with the agenda or outline of your presentation. The chart will help your audience see where you are taking them, and it will serve as a great visual reminder to you of what comes next. Knowing where you are in your presentation at all times will greatly reduce your anxiety.

The next step is to become comfortable with your venue. The more you make the unknowns about your environment known, the more at ease you will be. Whether you will be presenting from a pulpit, in a Bible study class, or in a living room, think through where people are going to sit, and even sit in their chairs to see what they will see or hear. Know your room. Walk it and know every corner of it from a presenter's perspective. If you have any control over the temperature of the room, make sure you know where the thermostat is located or that you have access to personnel who can make adjustments.

If you will be using equipment, test it out in advance, and then retest it right before your presentation to make sure it is working. Be prepared for equipment failure. Make extra copies of notes and handouts for insurance. Have a backup plan for everything, and know what you can skip if you are required to shorten your presentation. Also have some stand-by material ready, as well, just in case you run short. Most presentations run too long rather than too short, but it adds to your peace of mind if you know you will not end up with remaining minutes to fill with idle chatter.

One of the best ways to maximize your confidence and reduce nervousness is to rehearse your presentation a number of times. With each effective rehearsal, you become more comfortable and relaxed. It also allows you to anticipate and avoid challenges before they happen. Do a mental walk-through to familiarize yourself with the flow of your presentation. Then use your 3-D Outline™ to talk through your presentation and see how it flows verbally. Rehearse with the equipment and props you will be using so you can get used to them and ensure you are using them properly. Even rehearse in the same room if you can.

The night before your presentation, review your notes and run through your checklist to make sure everything is complete. Then get a good night's rest so you can be at your best! Arrive early at your venue so you can get things ready in advance. It shows your audience that you care, and it reduces your stress! If someone will be introducing you, be sure they have all the information about you they need.

Right before your presentation, review your checklist to make sure everything is done. You will be amazed at how your confidence level will soar and your anxiety level will go down when you see that it is! If you need it, though, give yourself a pep talk. Remind yourself that you have prepared thoroughly and that you can "do all things through Christ who strengthens" you. Then believe that you will do well and that your presentation will inspire and minister to your audience.

| STEP 5: OPEN WELL |

When you walk to the front of the room or greet people as they come into your class or your home, your smile should confidently suggest, "I am glad to be here." Anxiety is usually the highest at the start of a presentation. If you have carefully planned your opening, though, and you know it very well, you can get through the early part of your presentation with poise and assurance.

If possible, memorize your opening statement and have a clear plan for the transitions you need to make.

If you are using a microphone and you are still a little shaky, leave it on the mike stand instead of holding it in your hand during the first minute or two. If the quake in your voice is matching the quake in your hands, pause before starting. Look around the room, smile at a familiar face or two, rearrange your notes, adjust the microphone, and take a few deep breaths. Begin when you are ready. Avoid telling your audience that you are nervous. They may not have noticed, and your admission could cause them to scrutinize your presentation for signs of fear. Concentrate on breathing slowly and deeply to keep a steady supply of oxygen flowing.

Be yourself. In most presentation and ministry environments, your audience is rooting for you. *You* are the one that God has placed at the front of the room or at the head of the table at this time and place. So do not try to imitate anyone else. Just be the very best you that you can be.

Remember, you want to grab your audience's attention and get them involved immediately. Building rapport early helps boost your confidence and increases your audience's natural urge to want you to succeed. Use your visual aids or handouts, and ask them to write something down—it gets their eyes off of you and gives you a moment to get comfortable in the environment. If you are standing, you can move around and gesture to burn off nervous energy—it catches your audience's attention when you are animated. But avoid pacing like a caged tiger. Pause periodically to convey confidence.

It may surprise you to know that your audience may be nervous, too—especially if they don't know you or are not familiar with the environment. Almost every audience, however large or small, has four common, natural, and subconscious tensions. Knowing them and addressing them immediately in your presentation will not only alleviate them for your audience, but it will help you gain confidence as well. The four tensions exist between:

1. The audience and other audience members. Whether they know each other or not, have audience members get on their feet and shake hands and socialize with one another. Christians generally love to do this and may get carried away, so you may have to impose a time limit!

2. The audience and the presenter. This is especially true if the audience does not yet know you. Address this tension by building rapport, establishing and maintaining eye contact, smiling, and opening strong.

3. The audience and the materials. Audience members are naturally curious about handout materials. When they look through the materials, they sometimes stop listening to you. So do not hand them out until you need them. Address this tension by involving the audience with their materials as soon as you distribute them. Explain the handouts and ask your listeners to write their names on their materials.

4. The audience and the environment. Even if your audience is familiar with the room, you should make sure that the seats, temperature, and lighting are comfortable. Ask for feedback on the comfort issues, and then take care of any concerns. If a comfort issue is beyond your control, you may want to add a break or two to your agenda.

STEP 6: ENGAGE YOUR AUDIENCE

The more you can maintain the bond you establish with your audience, the more relaxed you will be. Involve them throughout your presentation. Ask them questions and encourage them to ask you questions. Speak to one person at a time, and make eye contact with everyone at least once if possible. When you know your audience members, call them by name. Get feedback from them by asking them how you are doing. Use *Strategic Engagement* tactics like games, stories, skits, or activities every five to seven minutes to keep them interested and smiling. Relax and have fun!

If you have planned a question and answer session at the end of your presentation, be sure to hold it before your summary. You want to be in control of your closing! To take any sting out of a question and answer session, think of it this way: Every question shows that there is interest in your presentation.

STEP 7: CLOSE WITH ACTION

By the time you get to the closing, you should be sailing. Nervousness should be a thing of the past. Now you need to help the audience feel good about what you shared and perhaps what they have learned. Leave them with something that will help them remember you and your message.

Have a clear closing that summarizes the main points of your presentation and proves that you have met your objectives and the audience's expectations. Be sure to include a call to action with a challenge to think or do something different as a result of what they heard.

Several years ago, when I was doing quite a bit of work with Wal-Mart, I went to the company's headquarters in Bentonville, Arkansas, to conduct some seminars. While I was there, I was asked to speak at one of the local churches about Bruce Wilkinson's book, *A Life God Rewards*. I knew there would be Wal-Mart executives there as well as executives from J. B. Hunt and some of my other client companies. So even though I have given hundreds of presentations to audiences of all sizes, I had a few butterflies. I just had to bring the butterflies into formation!

I was speaking about a great book with a powerful message, and I wanted to do my best for God. So I did the same things I have suggested in this chapter that you do. I wanted to know and really understand my audience, so I asked the person who was sponsoring me to tell me who would be attending. I asked him to give me any background information he could on the audience members and the church. I developed my 3-D Outline™, as I always do, and I was as prepared as I knew how to be. I got permission to go into the room early, and I prepared flip charts in advance and walked the room until I knew every corner of it. I tested all of the equipment. And as the people began coming in, I greeted them and spent some time getting to know them. By the time I was introduced and began my opening, I had my nervousness well under control.

Nervousness does not have to be your enemy. Make it work for you instead of against you by funneling back that nervous energy into your presentation in the form of enthusiasm. Prepare well. Focus on your presentation and your audience instead of on your fear, and learn to laugh at yourself. If you find humor in your mistakes, your audience will be much more at ease, and so will you!

Since the 3-D Outline™ plays such a major role in preparation and reducing nervousness, we are going to explore it in depth in the next chapter.

CHAPTER 2 VIP'S

! The most common reason people are nervous when it comes to presenting is the simple fact that they fear the unknown. Preparation—taking the unknown and turning it into the known—maximizes confidence.

! When you concentrate on why you are doing what you are doing, as opposed to what you are doing, your nervousness will begin to take a backseat.

! Take time before your presentation to find out about your audience and what their needs are. When your audience feels that you care about them, their warmth will melt your nervousness away.

! The number one rule in combating nervousness is "Do not procrastinate." Prepare early!

! As you gather your materials, gather "above and beyond" the actual content of your presentation.

! Anxiety is usually the highest at the start of a presentation. Carefully plan your opening and know it very well.

! The more you can maintain the bond you establish with your audience, the more relaxed you will be. Involve them throughout your presentation.

PREPARE

> The plans of the diligent lead to profit as
> surely as haste leads to poverty.

—PROVERBS 21:5

I have heard it said by pastors and church leaders that if you need something done in the church, ask someone who is already very busy. They are the ones who will get it done. Does that mean those of us who are busy and involved in church have a big "W" on our forehead—for Willing? Probably. When it comes to the things of God's kingdom, that is actually the right reputation to have.

Since you are reading this book, the odds are that you have been asked to take on a ministry role in the church or you are eager to do so. If so, it is likely that leaders of your church see you as one of the willing, and you are probably the type of person who is already really busy! I have good news for you. Whether this is all brand new to you or you have been making presentations for years, I can show you a quick and *simple* method that will help you stay focused and effectively prepare for your presentations by making the most of your time.

The step-by-step strategic thinking process we discussed in Chapter 1 will increase your effectiveness and help you save a tremendous amount of time. Rather than aimlessly trying to think up a presentation, you will be able to take deliberate steps that will culminate in a thorough and effective presentation. For many teachers and presenters, the most difficult step is figuring out the primary subject and focus of the presentation. By beginning with your objectives and sticking to them through the strategic thinking process, you will spend much less time staring at a blank screen or sheet of paper and be more effective in pulling your presentation together.

| THE POWERFUL 3-D OUTLINE™ |

I travel all over the world teaching sales people, managers, and executives how to be more effective in their presentations. Without fail, the 3-D Outline™ produces a tremendous amount of enthusiasm from novice presenters and seasoned pros alike. Speakers are drawn to the simple streamlining and preparation the 3-D Outline™ offers for *any* planned presentation.

We introduced this instrument in Chapter 1, and we'll be talking about it in each of the scenario chapters as well. As you interact with the 3-D Outline™ throughout this book, you will discover how powerful and simple it can be as you prepare to present to an audience of any size in any situation. Not only will the 3-D Outline™ allow you to present more effectively, it will also help you save time.

The 3-D Outline™ allows you to quickly get your arms around your presentation, because it helps you identify and quantify large amounts of information in a small amount of space and time. It uncovers many of the unknown elements of your presentation, helps you to see the big picture, and allows you to organize your thoughts and maintain your focus as you sort through your material.

Traditional presentation outlines—the ones we learned in school—are mostly one-dimensional. They describe *what* we want to say in a list of points and sub-points. That is where many people stop. When speakers focus only on the *what,* they easily get lost in tangents. They can become overwhelmed with all the possible directions a presentation can take, and they waste time gathering information that does not really fit with the presentation.

The 3-D Outline™ takes on two more dimensions that save countless hours in preparation. By helping speakers take a disciplined approach to all three dimensions of a presentation—the *what, why* and *how*—the 3-D Outline™ streamlines the speaker's focus. This approach encourages you to focus on your objectives and allow them to steer your presentation. By keeping your objectives (the *whys*) before you, you are forced to dissect the entire process and think about the techniques (the *hows*) you will use to inspire your audience, rather than focusing just on *what* you will deliver.

The 3-D Outline™ empowers you to estimate the amount of time you will need for each segment of your presentation. This simple practice will help you prepare the right amount of material. You'll be amazed at how much time and energy you save when you eliminate the worry of having enough content or stop developing segments for your presentation that will not fit into your allotted time. Using the 3-D Outline™ ensures that every major point in your presentation supports your objectives and justifies the time you have allotted for each segment.

Once you have the WHAT, WHY, and HOW columns completed, look at the TIME column and estimate how many minutes you will spend on each segment. Change this as often as you need to until it feels right. The body of your presentation usually consists of three to eight major points, and some may have sub-points. You may want to put an item on the end that has a variable time frame, just in case someone gets long-winded!

Look at a blank template for the 3-D Outline™ on the next page. Notice all of the information you can have at your fingertips on one sheet of paper. The top part of the outline allows you to write down virtually everything you need to remember, so you don't have to look for it in several different places, which helps you save time and eliminate stress.

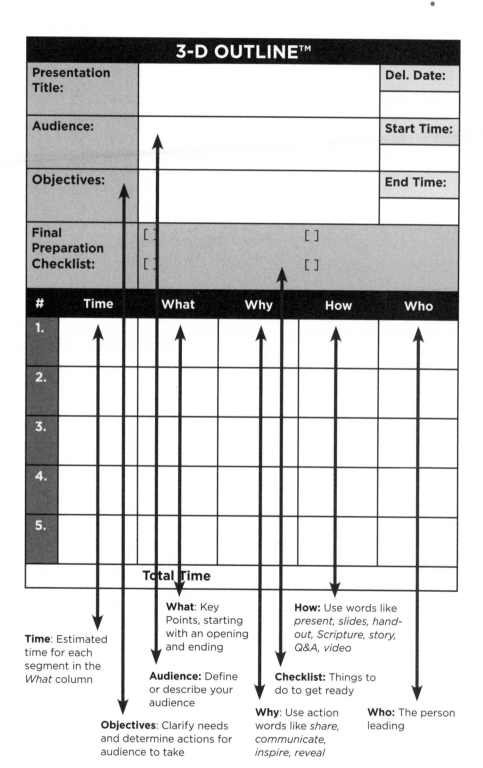

3-D OUTLINE™

Presentation Title:		Del. Date:
Audience:		Start Time:
Objectives:		End Time:

Final Preparation Checklist:	[ ] [ ]	[ ] [ ]

#	Time	What	Why	How	Who
1.					
2.					
3.					
4.					
5.					
	Total Time				

Time: Estimated time for each segment in the *What* column

What: Key Points, starting with an opening and ending

Audience: Define or describe your audience

Objectives: Clarify needs and determine actions for audience to take

How: Use words like *present, slides, hand-out, Scripture, story, Q&A, video*

Checklist: Things to do to get ready

Why: Use action words like *share, communicate, inspire, reveal*

Who: The person leading

Free templates for the 3-D Outline™ are available at www.PurposeFilled Presentations.com.

For clarification, let's do a quick review of the five columns, focusing on how they increase effectiveness and help save time.

! **What (The First Dimension):** The WHAT column identifies each segment of your presentation. Remember, this is where you will record a brief description of your introduction, opening, main points, and closing. Consider this column in conjunction with the WHY and TIME columns. When you develop only those segments that support your objectives and limit your preparation of each segment to the time parameters, you improve your effectiveness and save time.

! **Why (The Second Dimension):** The WHY column is for recording the reason why you have chosen what you will present. It helps you keep focused on your objective. By aligning every segment in the WHAT column with an objective in the WHY column, you will be able to see if you have too many objectives to support in the time allotted without diluting your presentation.

! **How (The Third Dimension):** The HOW column includes the method of delivery, such as talking, flip charts, PowerPoint, stories, testimonies, role-playing, games, activities, trivia, quizzes, videos, movie clips, or audio clips. Being aware of the time allotted for each segment in the WHAT column allows you to discern whether a delivery method you have chosen will fit with the other pieces of the puzzle. You will not over-prepare a PowerPoint presentation, for example, or plan a game *and* a video if you only have time for one or the other.

! **Time:** The TIME column is for recording the estimated amount of time you will have to cover each segment in the WHAT column. This feature allows you to limit your preparation to only what will fit into the time allotted. By spending a few minutes up front determining how much time you will spend on each segment, you won't spend needless hours and energy over-preparing material that simply will not fit.

! **Who:** The WHO column is an optional fifth element you can add if more than one person will be involved in the presentation delivery. By clearly defining in this segment who will cover what segment, each presenter will know what content they will need to gather and prepare.

With all of this information captured on one sheet of paper, your presentation can be designed, revised, and even delivered from this single document. Keep in mind that much is gained by simply getting your ideas down on paper. Just get started. You can change them later, if necessary, because nothing is set in stone.

All you need to produce this simple outline is a piece of paper, flip chart, or computer—or even a napkin. I was delighted at the resourcefulness of one client in Japan who created a 3-D Outline™ for a $250,000 project on the back of an airline ticket jacket!

As an added value for my readers, I have included sample 3-D Outlines™ on the *Purpose Filled Presentations* Web site (www.PurposeFilledPresentations.com) that you may download free of charge to help you save time as you shape your presentations. We have included sample outlines for a variety of ministry presentations. You should be able to download one that fits your presentation scenario and tweak it to fit your situation.

Let's look at a possible scenario and walk through the completion of a 3-D Outline™. Dean and Tiffany have recently been named missions coordinators for their church. They have a passion for missions and have been on several short-term mission trips. The youth minister has asked them to speak to the youth group at their church about an opportunity to go on a summer mission trip to South America. The teens would have to raise about $1500 each for this two-week trip. Although Dean and Tiffany are very enthusiastic about this trip, it is their first time to make such a presentation, and they are not sure how to go about it. They know they will have to make their presentation upbeat and exciting for the teenagers, using various media. Their objectives are to:

! Inspire the youth to respond to the call of short-term missions
! Present information about the need for missions work in South America
! Provide information about the trip and the planning meeting
! Ask the youth to join them on the missions trip
! Encourage the youth to commit to raising their own support

Dean and Tiffany's 3-D Outline™ may look something like this:

3-D OUTLINE™

Presentation Title:	Youth Mission Trip to South America	Del. Date:
		03/13
Audience:	Church Youth Group (Grades 9 through 12)	Start Time:
		7:00 PM
Objectives:	• Inspire for short-term missions • Present need in South America • Provide trip details • Gain preliminary commitment to trip and raising support	End Time:
		8:00 PM
Final Preparation Checklist:	[ ] Check projector equipment in youth hall [ ] Get brochures, prepare and copy handouts [ ] Call Sheri, Todd, and Jamie re giving testimonies [ ] Make sign-up sheet	

#	Time	What	Why	How	Who
1.	8	Opening: DVD on Teen Missions in South America	Inspire and present need	DVD	Dean
2.	7	Feedback and discussion	Create excitement and buy-in	Discussion	Dean, Tiffany, youth group
3.	10	Testimonies from past mission trips	Inspire	Testimonies	Sheri, Todd, and Jamie from youth group
4.	10	Details of trip and planning meeting	Provide details	Present handouts	Tiffany
5.	10	Questions and Answers	Satisfy concerns and create excitement	Discussion	Dean and Tiffany
6.	10	Closing and call to action	Get preliminary commitment	Present	Dean
7.	5	Prayer			Tiffany
	60 min.	**Total Time**			

That's it! It seems almost too simple. We have found, however, that this is an extremely valuable tool for both seasoned veterans and those who feel somewhat inadequate in front of an audience. There is only one catch: you have to actually do it. So grab a pencil and paper and give yourself ten or fifteen minutes to map out that presentation you have ahead of you. Then you will have time for that next ministry opportunity you've been asked to do!

| THE 3 Ps |

The opening and closing portions are possibly the most important part of any presentation. Preparing for these sections, however, can become a huge time-drain if you aren't focused or if you take the wrong approach. Rather than pulling the material for your opening from thin air, work on the opening and closing after the body of your presentation is nearly done.

In your opening, incorporate the 3 Ps: purpose, process, and payoff. Your audience wants to know the *purpose* of your presentation. Tell them why you are sharing with them. Are you exploring biblical accuracy about a particular topic? Are you showing how the Bible is still relevant today?

The audience will also appreciate knowing where you are going with the presentation or the *process* (agenda) you are taking them through. If you are leading a group meeting, help alleviate any anxiety of the unknown by telling them, "These are the three things I will be sharing with you." You'll find that including the process in your introduction will help you quickly develop a connection with your audience.

Finally, make sure you explain the *payoff* in your introduction. Audiences will want to know what they will be getting out of your presentation. Maybe you are offering a better understanding of a certain chapter of the Bible or a particular topic. Or perhaps you will empower a group to make accurate decisions based on new information about the church's financial condition.

Beginning your introduction with a creative method for sharing the purpose, process, and payoff will help you keep focused. The 3 Ps are attention-grabbers in and of themselves. When you use the 3 Ps in your opening, the first *what* in your 3-D Outline™ will look like this:

3-D OUTLINE™

Presentation Title:		Del. Date:
Audience:		**Start Time:**
Objectives:		**End Time:**

Final Preparation Checklist:	[ ] [ ]	[ ] [ ]

#	Time	What	Why	How	Who
1.		Opening: • Purpose (Objectives) • Process (Agenda) • Payoff (Benefit)			
2.					
3.					
4.					
5.					
		Total Time			

In Chapter 4 we will talk more about keeping your audience engaged and connected, and we will explore the practice of *Strategic Engagement*, a concept I have used for many years. I know you'll find it valuable.

CHAPTER 3 VIP'S

! The 3-D Outline™ uncovers many of the unknown elements of your presentation, helps you to see the big picture, and allows you to organize your thoughts and maintain your focus as you sort through your material.

! The three dimensions of a 3-D Outline™ are:

● What—This column identifies each segment of your presentation.
● Why—This column is for recording the reason why you have chosen what you will present.
● How—This column includes the method of delivery.

! The time column allows you to estimate the amount of time you will need for each segment and helps you prepare the right amount of material.

! By keeping your objectives (the whys) before you, you are forced to dissect the entire process and think about the techniques (the hows) you will use to inspire your audience, rather than focusing just on what you will deliver.

! The opening and closing portions are possibly the most important part of any presentation. In your opening, incorporate the 3 Ps: purpose (objectives), process (agenda), and payoff (benefits).

ENGAGE

| SO EVERYONE WINS |

A word aptly spoken is like apples of gold in settings of silver.

—PROVERBS 25:11

One balmy day in the South Pacific, a crewman on a navy ship spied smoke coming from one of three huts on an uncharted island. Upon arriving at the shore the crew was met by a shipwreck survivor. "I'm so glad you're here!" he said. "I've been alone on this island for five years!" The captain replied, "If you're all alone on the island, why do I see THREE huts?" The survivor said, "Oh. Well, I live in one and go to church in another." "What about the THIRD hut?" asked the captain. "That's where I USED to go to church."

People from several churches in your community have met together to discuss "maintaining unity in the body of Christ." Everyone laughed when you opened your presentation with this joke, and right off the bat you have successfully engaged your audience. You have created an atmosphere that allows them to enjoy the experience and benefit from it.

When people feel good about what they are experiencing, when they are complimented for their contributions, when they really get it, when they are touched by whatever you are sharing—they win! And when people win, they want to come back, they want to be involved, and they want to take that action or make that change that you are suggesting. Look for ways to let people win, and connection will happen!

I cannot emphasize enough the power of creating and maintaining a winning environment for your ministry audience. Remember, you are in service to the King of kings. Whether presenting in a church, in a home, or on a street corner, you are ministering to God's people. As 2 Corinthians 5:20 says, you are "Christ's ambassadors" when you are delivering any message on his behalf. When you put your audience in the winner's chair, you are observing Paul's admonition in Romans 12:10 to "honor one another above yourselves."

In Chapter 1 we introduced the *Seven Steps to Effective Presentations*. Under the sixth step, "Engage Your Audience," we talked about people wanting to be talked *with*, not *at*, and that a good presenter often speaks only about fifty percent of the time and facilitates involvement with the audience the rest of the time. We know that the average adult attention span is approximately five minutes, and that your audience is capable of thinking far faster than you can speak. So designing much of your presentation as a conversation with your audience is a great practice that keeps them involved and connected. Creating a conversational tone works well with almost any audience, regardless of size. Few people enjoy a presentation where the presenter tends to spend the entire time lecturing, yet everyone enjoys the inviting tone of a conversation.

The tone, or atmosphere, of your presentation affects the way your audience perceives your message. By creating an atmosphere that is enjoyable, inviting, and user-friendly, your audience is more likely to feel welcome, interested, and involved. And within that atmosphere, your audience is much more receptive to buying in to your presentation objective—whether it is to inspire, guide, persuade, or share knowledge.

To grab your audience members' attention and keep it, involve them in the presentation immediately. Call listeners by name (using nametags or name cards if you need to). Ask them questions, and give them opportunities to respond. Make them your partners in the presentation by asking them to share their expectations. You may want to write their responses on a flip chart and then come back to them at the end to show them you delivered. Or suggest that they write something down, like points of your presentation that are useful to them or questions they would like to ask at the end. Using handouts and providing highlighters is a fun way to get audience members involved. They can highlight their handouts with different colors to represent what they see as a takeaway for themselves or for someone else.

As you are going through your presentation, look around the room to make sure every member of your audience is connected. Maintain good eye contact, and be sure to stay aware of your body language, word choices, tonality, and enthusiasm. Remember that audience members have the ability to think a lot faster than you can talk, so their minds may wander. If you see someone who is not fully connected, you might call him by name and say, "Tell us a little about your thoughts on this."

By looking at people's faces in the audience and watching their body language, we can usually perceive their basic reaction to what we are doing. Sometimes we see audience members nodding their heads or even shouting out in agreement. I have been using two concepts for several years that engage the audience and provide input on the effectiveness of the presentation. The first is *"Verbal Surveying,"* and the other is what I have termed *"Target Polling."*

Verbal Surveying is simply asking the audience how things are going. Some people wait until the end of their presentations and then ask, "How did I do?" If you wait to gather feedback when the presentation is over, you will not be able to make mid-course adjustments. It is more effective to check in when you are about one-third of the way into your presentation. You can ask the members of your audience what they think, and then make necessary adjustments according to their responses. Ask simple questions like, "How are we doing?" and "Are we going too fast or slow?" "Is everything making sense, or should we go back to something?" "Does anyone have any questions on the things we have discussed so far?" This is a great tool for connecting with your audience, and it helps you deliver your best presentation.

In *Target Polling*, you poll people individually. You can mingle with the audience before your presentation and talk to people who have come early. Ask them to share their expectations for your time together. While you are mingling, get background information about the group, audience, or region. You can do *Target Polling* during a break as well. Make adjustments according to the feedback you get to fine-tune and improve the remainder of your presentation.

Another great strategy is to create peaks of interest. At the beginning or even throughout your presentation, you give your audience teasers about something that is coming up and create a heightened interest about where you are going. You might say something like, "In a little bit, we are going to talk about some exciting things that are coming up for our group." Foreshadowing thoughts and ideas that are coming up triggers your audience's curiosity. If you have planned something that is on their minds or something that relates to their world, let them know it is coming. Newscasters often do this just before a station break.

They know foreshadowing effectively hooks the audience and keeps them watching. Just be sure to deliver what you foreshadow.

You want all of these things to happen in the natural flow of your presentation. Be sure to choose things from these suggestions that fit your style and personality. Be yourself and avoid borrowing techniques that make you appear stilted or unnatural. Make certain that you consider your audience's sense of humor and style when you create teasers and hooks.

Not long ago I was listening to a guest speaker in our church, an attorney, who impressed me with his ability to engage his audience and create a great winning environment. I have to confess that at first I was skeptical. He had placed four flip charts on the stage—before a congregation of one thousand people! I thought, *What is this guy doing? You don't use flip charts for an audience this size!* I knew that he was a great presenter, but I just didn't know how he was going to pull it off.

His message actually consisted of four separate, specific points. With each point, he did a great job of facilitating and engaging the audience, getting them to boil that point down to one word. He had them repeat the word, and then he walked back to the first flip chart and wrote the first letter of that word in very large print. He then continued on to the next point, the next word, and the next letter. He repeated that four times, until the four letters on his flip charts spelled out one word that powerfully reinforced his message. It was a very effective way to pull his audience in.

| STRATEGIC ENGAGEMENT |

Remember this formula: On average, people retain about ten percent of what they read, twenty percent of what they hear, thirty percent of what they see, fifty percent of what they hear and see, seventy percent of what they say, and *ninety percent of what they say and do.* It follows, then, that if you want your audience to act on one out of every ten words you say, gear your presentation toward a lecture, where they are just listening to what you say. On the other hand, if you want them to be inspired by nine out of ten words you say, get them thoughtfully involved in saying and doing it themselves. That is "*Strategic Engagement.*"

Used correctly, *Strategic Engagement* can be one of the most effective tools for creating a winning atmosphere for your audience. The degree to which people enjoy an experience usually has a direct bearing on how well they absorb it and take appropriate action. Simply put, *Strategic Engagement* is activity that breaks up the monotony of hearing one speaking voice and *makes a point* with something other than words. It revitalizes your audience and adds the "fun factor."

The Internet holds a wealth of material that you can use for *Strategic Engagement*. There are some great Web sites out there for Christian jokes, like *www.jokes.christiansunite.com*. Telling a joke is one way to get people to laugh and lighten up. The only problem is that many people aren't blessed with the ability to tell jokes well. If you are not gifted in that area, perhaps you should steer away from jokes. You might also find some great one-line quotes on the Web, or you can purchase a book of quips and quotes. Encourage contributions from those extroverts in your group with the gift of humor. When they get people laughing, the entire group wins.

Games, skits, activities, and events are great forms of *Strategic Engagement*, because they get your audience members up and moving. Use a little friendly competition to *really* wake up the room! Video clips also help your audience connect.

I have used dozens of different techniques for *Strategic Engagement* over the years. The following eight techniques have proven to be no-fail tools for my presentations:

1. Use a guest speaker from the audience. Ask a person from your audience to come up and participate in the presentation. He could give a testimony or tell about his experience or expertise with the topic you are discussing. At the appropriate point in your presentation, simply invite him to share what he knows. Make certain you talk with your guest speaker before your presentation. Clearly explain what you want the speaker to share and how long he should take. The guest speaker should enhance your presentation. He should not overrun it. So make certain you give him a small window of time.

2. If you are presenting to a large group, take your microphone and walk around the audience while calling for volunteers to add some input on your topic, share a thought, or answer a question. Your effort will create a unique level of involvement and connection between you and your audience. This is a great way to get the eyeballs off of you for a few minutes to give yourself some breathing space.

3. If you are presenting to a small group, give everyone a chance to speak. For example, you could say, "Let's go around the room, and I would like for each of you to spend about thirty seconds and comment on the subject."

4. Have audience members discuss something with their neighbors. When you need a break, you might say, "Why don't we take a minute or two for you to get with a person who is right next to you and discuss this idea. Then after a couple of minutes we'll come back together and talk about your conclusions." There is no faster way to give everyone a chance to talk and personally engage in your presentation. This usually brings a new level of excitement and involvement to your audience.

5. Have a planned small group activity where your audience members break out into small groups. They can answer questions that you have written out, go through a flip chart that you have developed as a group during your presentation, or search out something from the Bible. Have each group select one person to share an important idea the group discussed.

6. Have a contest. You might divide the room into sections and see which group can come up with the most Scriptures on a particular subject. Or if you are talking to couples about marriage, you may see which group can come up with the most creative date ideas for married couples.

7. Play trivia. If you give multiple-choice answers for trivia, poll the audience to see how many people voted for each possible answer. If time allows, you can have a person share the rationale behind his answers.

8. Take the trivia to the next level, and give a quiz. You can hand out the questions to someone or to the whole group, and then have everyone participate in filling in the answers. This strategy provides an opportunity for relationship-building between audience members and fosters involvement in your presentation.

Regardless of the types of *Strategic Engagement* you use in your presentation, there are some basic principles you should follow to avoid common pitfalls and problems with these creative ideas:

1. Be prepared. Know what activities you want to use well in advance of your presentation. If you expect your audience to participate, always

explain the directions clearly and check for understanding. You don't want people feeling nervous or ill at ease because they don't know what to do.

2. Be sure to give the participants a clear idea of the purpose behind each activity. When they know the purpose, they are more likely to join in enthusiastically.

3. Help keep things loose by participating in the activities along with the attendees. Some of the ideas listed above require a relaxed atmosphere and a sense of humor. Your audience will be much more apt to join in wholeheartedly if you seem relaxed and comfortable doing the activities.

These ideas will help you engage your audience and create winning environments for your presentations. Several years ago I wrote a couple of books that may be helpful to you as you plan your ministry presentations. *Icebreakers* is a great resource for both opening activities and Strategic Engagement, and *Speaking Spice* contains stories and anecdotes that you can use either to open your presentations or to drive home a point. I have modified some of those activities and stories for ministry settings and have included them in our resource section in Part 3 of this book. Feel free to use them in your presentations.

In Part 1 of this book, we have shared the basic presentation skills that apply to Christian communicators. Communication is a gift from God. We can become better ministers for him and increase our presentation effectiveness if we apply proven practices and good processes. The seven basic steps that I share in this book will help you prepare well, move away from nervousness and toward confidence, and create a winning atmosphere for your audiences. As we move on to Part 2, I will help you apply many of these best practices in various ministry scenarios to help you become a more confident, effective ambassador for Christ.

CHAPTER 4 VIP'S

! Designing much of your presentation as a conversation with your audience keeps them involved and connected.

! Create an atmosphere that is enjoyable, inviting, and user-friendly, so your audience will feel welcome, interested, and involved.

! To grab your audience members' attention and keep it, involve them in the presentation immediately.

! *Verbal Surveying* is simply asking the audience how things are going. Perodically, ask the members of your audience what they think, and then make necessary adjustments throughout your presentation.

! *Target Polling* is polling people individually, either before the presentation or during a break. Ask audience members to share their expectations, ideas, and suggestions, and then make adjustments accordingly.

! Create peaks of interest to foreshadow things you will talk about and trigger your audience's curiosity.

! *Strategic Engagement* is activity that breaks up the monotony of hearing one's speaking voice and *makes a point* with something other than words. It revitalizes your audience and often adds the "fun factor."

PART

2

APPLYING THE BASICS

SHARE YOUR TESTIMONY

> But in your hearts set apart Christ as Lord. Always be prepared to give an answer to everyone who asks you to give the reason for the hope that you have. But do this with gentleness and respect.

—1 PETER 3:15

One of the most amazing testimonies of all times is recorded for us in the twenty-sixth chapter of the book of Acts, where the apostle Paul is speaking to King Agrippa:

On one of these journeys I was going to Damascus with the authority and commission of the chief priests. About noon, O king, as I was on the road, I saw a light from heaven, brighter than the sun, blazing around me and my companions. We all fell to the ground, and I heard a voice saying to me in Aramaic, "Saul, Saul, why do you persecute me? It is hard for you to kick against the goads." Then I asked, "Who are you, Lord?" "I am Jesus, whom you are persecuting," the Lord replied. "Now get up and stand on your feet. I have appeared to you to appoint you as a servant and as a witness of what you have seen of me and what I will show you. I will rescue you from your own people and from the Gentiles. I am sending you to them to open their eyes and turn them from darkness to light, and from the power of Satan to God, so that they may receive forgiveness of sins and a place among those who are sanctified by faith in me." —Acts 26:12-18

What an amazing account of events! And that's what a testimony is—a true account or story. Everyone has a story, but Christian testimonies are unique and even sacred. A Christian testimony is an account of what our holy God has done in an earthly life. If you are a Christian, you have a Christian testimony. In its abbreviated form, your testimony is the story of how you came to be a follower of Christ. But your complete testimony includes all that God has done in your life since that time. Your testimony is a story that begins with your first stirrings of recognition of the God of the universe. It weaves through the changes that brought you to an understanding or recognition of your need for a Savior, and it continues in what God is doing in your life today.

As a Christian, you may be called upon to tell your story from time to time. Someone may casually ask, "So, how did you come to know the Lord?" Or you may be invited to share your testimony before a group or audience. You may have time to prepare, or it may be an impromptu invitation. On other occasions, you may feel led to share your testimony with someone. You may find that your testimony fits perfectly into a conversation you have while on an airplane or talking with a new friend or sharing a barbecue with your next-door neighbor. You may be on the phone with someone who is going through a difficult situation when you realize that your testimony would comfort and encourage that person.

Scripture challenges us in 2 Timothy 4:2 to be prepared "in season and out of season" to preach, correct, rebuke, and encourage. And 1 Peter 3:15 reminds us to always be prepared to give the reason for the hope we have. Our testimonies are stories of God's work and transforming power in our lives. He uses those stories to bring light and hope to those who don't know him and to encourage those who do.

Your story is powerful evidence of God's work. So wouldn't you want to present your testimony with as much clarity and impact as possible? With a little preparation you can always be ready to tell someone what God has done in your life.

I am not asking you to be prepared to drone out a canned presentation or remove the emotion and spontaneity from a conversation. An effective testimony should always come from the heart so that it can go straight into the hearts of the audience. But a little preparation and forethought can help you present your story with effectiveness and intensity. Investing time in preparing your testimony now will help you find a comfortable way to optimize the opportunity to make an impact when it comes.

As you are formatting your testimony, it's good to identify *anchor points* of your story. Anchor points are key landmarks within your testimony that help you take your story from one point to the next. Identifying anchor points affords you a level of comfort even in impromptu situations. You just need to remember those landmarks and start talking from one to the next. The degree of intimacy and detail you incorporate between anchor points will vary depending on your audience and circumstances.

I have three primary anchor points in my story. The first is my friendship with a boy named David Peak. His family moved onto my block when I was about four years old. The first time I met David, he was riding his bicycle in front of my house, and he had a flat tire. I told him that my grandfather owned a service station and that we would get the tire fixed right up. That was the fortuitous beginning of a great friendship—one that would forever change my life.

David's father was disabled and confined to a wheelchair, but he did not let that stop him for a moment. As David and I grew older, his dad taught us how to play golf, play basketball, and bowl—all from a wheelchair! Sitting in the car at the golf course, he walked us through the mechanics of golfing by using binoculars and walkie-talkies. He had a special basketball court built in his backyard where he taught us to shoot hoops. Our bowling alley had steps at the front, so David and I and two of our friends would lift his wheelchair and carry him inside. As far as I know, he was America's only wheelchair-bound bowling coach, but he was a good one. Needless to say, Mr. Peak had a profound influence on my life. But it was more than the great friendship he modeled for me. I believe God orchestrated the friendship and its timing to set me up for the most important event of my life.

My family and I attended church, but none of us really had a personal relationship with the Lord. When I was thirteen years old, David and his father invited me to attend their church—which brings me to my second anchor point: church camp.

Within a few months after I started attending church with the Peak family, I was invited to attend summer youth camp. Nestled in the Arbuckle Mountains of southern Oklahoma is a wonderful camp called Falls Creek. It is surrounded by beautiful trees and rustic wilderness. I made some great friends from various churches and backgrounds. And I enjoyed the nurturing and caring counselors and ministers at the camp. During one of the programs, I responded to an invitation and asked Jesus to be the Lord of my life. Even though I was thirteen, I meant it with all my heart. You won't be surprised to know that Jesus said yes, and he has never left me since.

Because of severe financial setbacks, I went through some pretty traumatic times in my twenties. Those difficulties have become the third anchor point in my testimony. I had let my commitment to God slip a little by that time, but God used the incredible loss and turmoil to reclaim my attention. I may have lost millions of dollars, but I gained something much more valuable when I recommitted my life to Christ. God was my anchor during those difficult times, and he led me to a new level of spiritual maturity through them.

My story is not incredibly unique or overtly miraculous. It does not have cliffhanger plot twists. But my story is powerful because it is true. It has made me who I am today, and it continues to shape almost everything I do. Your story may be fantastic or commonplace. Either way, I guarantee that it has power to change lives. If you will take the time to think about how God got hold of your life and define the anchor points of your story, you will be amazed at how God will use it to help others.

I have had opportunities through the years to share my testimony, and I believe God has used it to encourage many people. Both of my girls have come to know the Lord, and I have helped them shape their testimonies to share with others, as well. In fact, my twelve-year-old daughter, Paige, had such an opportunity just a few days before this chapter was written. I will use her recent story as our example as we go through the *Seven Steps to Effective Presentations* to help you design your testimony for maximum impact.

| Step 1: Clarify Objectives |

Your objectives for sharing your testimony in an impromptu situation may be as varied as your opportunities. Do you want to encourage or inspire someone? Do you want your audience to start thinking about spiritual things? Or do you want to present an opportunity for the person to start following Christ? Sometimes your objective may be to simply complete what you feel God wants you to do! Taking a moment to say a quick prayer and think about your objective before you jump into your impromptu testimony may have a big impact on the outcome.

If you have been invited to share your testimony with a group and you have time to plan, you obviously have more of an opportunity to pray and think through your objectives. If you have not received such an invitation, you may want to focus on the objective of being prepared for impromptu opportunities.

There may be times when you feel led to include an account of the gospel in your impromptu testimony. Find a method that is easy for you to remember and easy for others to understand. Janet Folger, the president of Faith2Action, recalls how James Kennedy, the founder and senior minister of the Coral Ridge Presbyterian Church in Fort Lauderdale, Florida, was prepared to explain the heart of Christianity during an impromptu opportunity. "I remember one time he shared the gospel over lunch using his silverware. Pointing to a knife on a napkin representing the letter 'I,' he proclaimed, 'That's every religion in the world except Christianity—what must *I* do? How can *I* earn my way to heaven? *I* need, *I* should, *I* must.' He then placed a fork over the knife to form a cross and said, 'Christianity is the only religion in the world about what God did to reach man and make a way for us to be with him.'" [5]

Dr. Kennedy used a very simple presentation to make a profound point. It's likely that your story will cause others to seek greater understanding of your faith. To be prepared for every opportunity, consider including a simple explanation about what Christ has done for you as one of your objectives.

STEP 1 | EXAMPLE

My daughter Paige accepted the Lord when she was ten years old. Her story is a little unique in that the Lord gave her two dreams that actually led to her conversion. She had the dreams two weeks apart and both came prior to her decision to give her life to Christ.

The first dream was longer and more involved. Satan and Jesus came to our house disguised as salesmen. Satan ended up chasing Paige all over the house, but when they ran into her mom and Jesus, the dream ended. In her second dream, she was living her normal life except that she was clearly a Christian.

When Paige awoke from her second dream, she went to talk to her mom and tell her about the dreams. When her mom asked what she thought they meant, Paige replied, "I think Jesus is telling me that he is knocking on my heart and asking me to let him come in." And she did.

Both of my daughters attend a great Christian school. When Paige was in kindergarten, her older sister Brooke and some of Brooke's friends went to her class to share their testimonies. Recently, Paige was praying and felt that God was leading her to share her testimony with the kindergarten class at her school, as well. The teacher was thrilled.

It was a wonderful privilege for me to help Paige prepare to share her testimony. She wasn't quite sure what an objective was, but she explained that she had several reasons for wanting to share:

! She felt that God had asked her to share, and she wanted to obey.
! She wanted to minister to this kindergarten class the same way her sister had ministered to her some years earlier.
! She wanted to tell the kids to start listening for God's "knock" on their hearts.

| STEP 2: DEFINE YOUR AUDIENCE |

It's just as important to consider your audience when giving your testimony as it is for any other presentation. You can be certain that your audiences will be varied over a lifetime of sharing. Each time you share, be sure to ask the Lord for guidance. He may lead you to place emphasis on one aspect of your testimony to meet the needs of your audience.

If you are sharing your testimony for a large group with people who are at different levels in their spiritual walk, your objective may be to help everyone understand that God can change anyone. You may want to share your testimony with a person in your small group who needs encouragement or with a new friend as you get to know each other. You may be invited to share a short version of your story with your Sunday school class or Bible study to support the theme of the lesson.

It is important to consider the age of your audience. If I planned to share my testimony with children or youth, my objective may be to relate my testimony to something they are familiar with, such as a movie, a song, or a game. If I planned to share my testimony with a group of thirteen-year-old boys, I may relate to them on their level by emphasizing the fun I had at summer camp and the friends I made. If I plan to present to a group of dads, I may focus on the impact that Mr. Peak had on my life to help them understand the power of their influence.

STEP 2 | EXAMPLE

Paige knew the age of her audience, but she only knew one little boy personally—the brother of a friend. She knew that they all attended a Christian school and that most of them came from Christian homes. Because of that, she could assume that most of them already had at least some familiarity with the gospel. So Paige decided to concentrate more on helping the children think about their own response to Jesus' sacrifice rather than concentrating on what he did.

| STEP 3: GATHER CONTENT |

For the most part, your content is going to come from your heart and your memory. As you gather the details of your testimony, consider the moments and events that bring it to life in your memory. Sometimes it helps, both in the recalling and in the retelling, to touch the different senses. Thinking through the following questions may spark memories for you and can add rich detail to your testimony:

- **!** What were you seeing? In my case, it was the beautiful setting among the trees.
- **!** Do you remember a particular smell? For me, it was the smell of the outdoors.
- **!** What were you feeling physically? Was the weather hot or cold? I remember the refreshing breeze on a hot summer evening.
- **!** What were you feeling emotionally? I felt the thrill of a brand new relationship with God.
- **!** What were the sounds around you? I heard a guitar playing and the campers singing.
- **!** Was there a taste involved? I remember the delicious meals at camp.

Write these things down as you pull them from your memory. It's important to also consider the history that brought you to the place of decision or that moved you along in your journey. Identify your anchor points. If you can remember a clear point of decision, be sure to include the thoughts and emotions you experienced as you wrestled with it.

The last thing you want to do is bore people with the details of your story and all of your challenges and victories. Share enough detail to help your audience have a context for your story and to understand that your experience was real. If time permits, it's good to talk about at least a few of the things God has led you through to build your faith and accomplish spiritual maturity in your life.

STEP 3 | EXAMPLE

Paige had written down her testimony shortly after her conversion be-cause the minister had asked that she share her testimony when she was baptized. She got that paper out and reviewed it to gather content for this occasion. She also knew, of course, that I had made a few presentations myself and had shared my testimony. So she asked me to help her think through some other points as well. We talked about the emotions she felt during her dreams, the environment she remembered as she spoke with her mother, and the thoughts she had as she decided to follow Christ.

| STEP 4: MAXIMIZE PREPARATION |

Even though you know all the details of your testimony, write it down. You don't want to read it to your audience, and you likely won't need to since it is your story. Writing it down, however, will help you see if it makes sense to your audience and if it flows well. I encourage you to complete at least a light version of the 3-D Outline™ so you can work from that during your presentation. It will help you think through all three dimensions so you will have a mental image of how it is all going to take place. If you are preparing for an impromptu presentation, reviewing your 3-D Outline™ from time to time will keep your presentation sharp when the opportunity arises.

Do as much as you can to make the unknowns known. Familiarize yourself with the room, test the equipment, stand where you will be standing, and sit in the chairs where your audience will be sitting. Rehearse your testimony in front of a friend or family member, if possible. Speaking through it a couple of times will increase your confidence. If you are preparing for an impromptu presentation, have your practice audience ask you questions that come to mind while you present.

STEP 6 | EXAMPLE

I was proud of Paige's creativity when she told me she wanted to give lollipops to the kids. She figured the lollipops would serve as a tangible reminder of her testimony and would help her make a connection that lasted beyond her presentation.

| STEP 7: CLOSE WITH ACTION |

You can almost always close with prayer after you share your testimony. If your objective is to lead your audience to the Lord or into a deeper walk with the Lord, you may want to ask for a response. Offer to pray with anyone who wants to grow closer to God.

If prayer or an invitation to accept Christ doesn't seem like an appropriate closing, you may want to allow time for questions. The questions people ask may help you pinpoint where they are in their faith and may also reveal how they are reacting to your testimony. Look for opportunities to follow up with individuals who seem especially curious or interested.

STEP 7 | EXAMPLE

Paige closed her testimony by telling the kindergartners that God wants them to follow after him, and she encouraged them to listen for God's knock on their hearts.

Your testimony is one of the most important presentations you can give, as it can have eternal results. Take time to prepare now for planned or impromptu opportunities to share your spiritual journey. You never know when or how God will use you.

SCENARIO 1 VIP'S

! Our testimonies are stories of God's work and transforming power in our lives. He uses those stories to bring light and hope to those who don't know him and to encourage those who do.

! Anchor points are key points within your testimony that help you tell your story from one point to the next. Identifying anchor points affords you a level of comfort even in impromptu situations.

! There may be times when you feel led to include an account of the gospel in your impromptu testimony. Find a method that is easy for you to remember and easy for others to understand.

! Consider including a simple explanation about what Christ has done for you as one of your objectives.

! As you gather the details of your testimony, consider the moments and events that bring it to life in your memory.

! A good way to open when you are sharing your testimony is to give some background information and history that led to your current faith.

! Be sensitive to the flow of your testimony and what God may be doing through it. Subtle techniques like varying your volume, a dramatic pause, facial expressions, and body movements can make a big impact.

! You can almost always close with prayer after you share your testimony. Offer to pray with anyone who wants to grow closer to God.

5. Information in this section was taken from Craig von Buseck, "Dr. D. James Kennedy, 1930–2007," CBN.com, *http://www.cbn.com/spirituallife/churchandministry/vonbuseck_D_James_Kennedy_Dies.aspx* (accessed October 20, 2005).

SCENARIO

2

HOST A WORSHIP SERVICE

> " Just as each of us has one body with many members, and these members do not all have the same function, so in Christ we who are many form one body, and each member belongs to all the others. We have different gifts, according to the grace given us. If a man's gift is prophesying, let him use it in proportion to his faith. If it is serving, let him serve; if it is teaching, let him teach; if it is encouraging, let him encourage; if it is contributing to the needs of others, let him give generously; if it is leadership, let him govern diligently; if it is showing mercy, let him do it cheerfully. "
>
> **—ROMANS 12:4-8**

My good friend, Buz Barlow, an attorney who has worked with both World Vision and Dr. Robert Schuller, was recently asked to deliver a message for the sixtieth anniversary celebration of the church he attended for most of his life. Buz was trained in law, not theology, and all five of the church's previous pastors were in the congregation while he was speaking. Talk about pressure! He had prepared well, and he was pretty confident that his presentation hit its mark. He later shared with me that he believed the secret to his success was how he handled the first three minutes. Within those first few moments he touched his audience by relating two things that connected with virtually every person there.

Most of the people in the congregation fondly remembered his daughter, who had grown up in that church. He shared with them that the little girl they remembered had entered into full-time ministry as an adult, and that her fiancé had recently proposed to her in church. Then he told them that his mother, who was in the audience, was celebrating her eighty-seventh birthday that day. The audience warmed to him immediately, his confidence soared, and he was able to deliver his presentation with ease.

This chapter is for all of you who are not trained pastors but find yourselves delivering a presentation during a worship service for various other reasons. Perhaps, like my friend Buz, you have been asked to do a special one-time presentation. Or maybe you attend a smaller church and your pastor has become ill or has an emergency situation. Perhaps you have been asked to deliver some of the elements that take place before or after the sermon, such as the welcome, announcements, the offering, or communion.

Since one of the latter opportunities is most likely, we will focus on making presentations that support or enhance the sermon, rather than on preparing the sermon. It would be helpful if anyone who has any role in the oversight, orchestration, or implementation of the worship service in your church would read this chapter. Church staff members and worship leaders could benefit, as well as volunteers, as this chapter will help bring a tight cohesiveness to the service that will allow for the most valuable use of time. The more you all work together as a team, the more effective your overall ministry will be.

When you present to the entire church, you are an important representative of your church to visitors. Remember that your presentation may in part help guide people as they make their decision on where or if they attend church. As an up-front communicator, you have the responsibility of *leading* the people in your congregation to take the next step. You may be leading them to take action on a specific announcement, give in the offering, greet each other, or make a change in their lives. When you understand that you are *leading* up front, it changes the way you communicate. It shifts the focus from you to the people you are leading. Understanding your role makes you more aware of your objectives as you lead the people of your church from one place to another.

God works through people. Your role is critical. You are serving as one of the primary faces and voices of your church. So do well the things that a good host does, such as:

! Puts people at ease, provides explanation, and clarifies expectations
! Encourages people to engage in the experiences of worship
! Helps connect the elements of the service together
! Helps visitors relax and feel welcome

! Points people in the right direction after the service if they have questions or need more information.

Suppose you spend ten minutes leading your congregation to take action in the activities you are announcing. If you are speaking to a congregation of one hundred, you have actually had one thousand total minutes of direct communication or "face time" with your audience. When you think of the reach and impact you can have when you present to an audience, you can see that you have an incredible opportunity and a big responsibility each time you present! It's worth every second you invest in reading this book and improving your effectiveness. It is worth every prayer. Your ministry is worthwhile no matter how much of the service you are responsible for.

I hope you will take your role seriously and understand the impact you can have on people's lives. Sharpen your skills by implementing the principles in the following *Seven Steps to Effective Presentations*.

| STEP 1: CLARIFY OBJECTIVES |

Before you plan what you are going to say and do during the worship service, you need to define the objectives that will drive your words and actions. Someone on the church's leadership team will more than likely provide some beginning direction and parameters for you. Let's look at the various elements involved in hosting or supporting the service and consider some possible objectives:

! Welcome

- Greet the audience and help them feel good about the decision they made to come to church.
- Invite people to greet and introduce themselves to one another.
- Help people focus on God and disengage from worries, concerns, and to-do lists.
- Help people tune in to what God wants to do in them.
- Preview the service.
- Ask God to work during your service.

! Announcements

- Invite involvement in congregational events and various ministry opportunities.

- Provide ways for people to connect more deeply with others during the week.
- Encourage people to get involved in events that can change lives.
- Invite and provide instruction for guest registration.
- Inform, update, and educate the congregation regarding special projects or events.

! Offering

- Communicate that offering is an act of worship.
- Offer simple instructions on how to participate.
- Explain the expectations for participation.
- Provide scriptural support for giving.

! Communion

- Celebrate the life, death, and resurrection of Jesus.
- Help people respond to Christ's instruction.
- Offer instructions about what communion is, why it is important, and how to participate.
- Reflect on one or more of the many aspects of this act of worship, such as grace, hope, joy, and God's character.

! Introduction of the pastor or speaker

- Provide background information.
- Create a connection.
- Build anticipation.

! Closing the Service

- Help tie the whole worship experience together.
- Invite people back the following week.

STEP 1 | EXAMPLE

Chris, who has served for several years as a worship host in a medium-sized church, believes that the role of worship host is becoming more prevalent. "Service hosting is a relatively new role," he said, "and one that has traditionally been filled by the worship leader or a staff pastor."

Chris believes that the service host's objectives should tie into the core values or clearly defined vision or mission statement of the church. He said, "One of the three core values at our church is community, and we are constantly looking for ways to get people to connect. Often when I give an announcement, I tie it back to that core value. For example, I might say, 'We have a new small group that is meeting at John Smith's house on Tuesday nights. It is very important to have close relationships in the church with people you can actually name, and we encourage you to get involved.' Another of our church's core values is grace, so it's pretty easy to pull that into the communion meditation if that's where I'm hosting, because grace is the whole reason for the church's existence. When the church's mission or core values are reinforced by someone who is not paid staff, it is really valuable."

Chris identifies more specific objectives for each element of the service he is asked to lead. "Let's say I am asked to do the communion meditation," he said. "The first objective is to clarify what communion is all about—remembering and honoring Christ's sacrifice for us. Another objective is to craft everything I say to drive home the main point of the message. I gather as much information as I can about the theme for the day, the title of the message, and the Scripture reference. Let's say I found that the message was going to be about Christ's humility, out of Philippians chapter two. I might share a personal experience I had that week that revealed my pride to me. Then I may say something like, 'That experience got me thinking about how incredible it was that Jesus left the glory of heaven to become a flesh and blood man and humble himself to death, even the most cursed death, the death on the cross.' My objective was to help people connect with Christ's sacrifice in a way that tied in with the theme of the message—humility."

| STEP 2: DEFINE YOUR AUDIENCE |

It is important to keep in mind that whether you are delivering to a congregation of fifty, five hundred, or five thousand, you are not speaking to a crowd, but to a collection of *individuals*. Think of it as having a conversation with individuals from the front of the church. Remember that each individual is at a different stage in his or her journey of faith in Christ. Knowing your audience and understanding its needs are crucial to knowing how to satisfy those needs.

One important aspect of knowing your audience is learning to be sensitive to the mood of the service. There are so many variables to take into account that you may have to adjust your plan in order to be sensitive to the moment. Rely on the Holy Spirit to help you "read the room" so you can take advantage of the significant moments in the service and not ruin them by pulling or pushing in a different direction.

Was that last worship song reverent or one of celebration? Is there a sense of awe in the room or expectation? When you give your presentation, acknowledge the moment through what you say and then make the transition to the next part of the service. For example, you may need to offer a prayer *before* you crack that great joke you were planning. Or if something funny just happened, acknowledge it before you move into the more serious topic that's coming next.

It is equally important for you to be sensitive to the tone or personality of your church and your pastor. Is your congregation more receptive to a casual atmosphere and humor than they are to a more formal worship experience? Do they enjoy the use of props or theatrics? I am not suggesting that you assume a delivery style that is not really you, because God wants you to be real in every situation. But you can be creative and still match the personality of your church by making a few minor adjustments. Your opportunity to present should support and enhance the rest of the service. Your time in front of the congregation is not the place to make a statement regarding the culture of the church or the leadership. Rather it is an opportunity to support your leaders and to unify the congregation.

Remember that your presentation may go well beyond the people you are speaking to. Listeners may relate what they heard to others. Some may download a podcast of the service or play a recording. If your church records or distributes your worship services, you may need to consider how your presentation will impact outside audiences.

STEP 2 | EXAMPLE

"Defining your audience is huge," Chris said. "When you are talking to a group of people, there are a couple of things going on. You have a range of spiritual maturity—from people who aren't sure they believe any of this or are sure they *don't* believe any of this, to people who have been following Christ for years. The second thing is that the people in your audience are all over the map emotionally. Some people may have had the best week of their lives, and some may have had the worst week of their lives. Some people feel very good about their relationship with God; others are feeling very guilty and broken.

"Obviously, I can't target all of those groups of people with one communion meditation. I would probably focus on one. But I may pull several of those groups in when I pray, saying something like, 'Lord, in a room this size there are people who are having the best week of their lives and there are those who are having the most difficult week of their lives. You know what's going on with all of them. I pray that during these next couple of minutes of meditation, you meet each of us where we are.'

"I might address the different spiritual maturity levels by saying, perhaps in the welcome, 'If you've come here today not sure if you believe any of this, please don't feel any pressure to participate. If you've come here and your faith is feeling kind of shaky, but you're trying to believe, know that you only need the tiniest bit of faith to begin following Christ.' Even a quick mention like that can make someone feel like they belong here because we understand where they are.

"I think it's important to remember your audience when you're making announcements, too. If I'm announcing a new married couples' group or something similar, I usually acknowledge the groups of people to whom that announcement doesn't apply."

| STEP 3: GATHER CONTENT |

Before you start gathering the material for your presentation, find out what involvement your pastor or designated staff person wants in the process. Most churches have way too many things going on to announce all of them. Many churches have preset criteria for determining which announcements should be made. Churches may also have denominational guidelines for communion, offering, and other areas you may support. Some ministers may prefer to approve your presentation before you give it. You may also need to work with the technical team or church office staff to coordinate graphic slides or bulletin announcements.

Sometimes a presentation may be related to the direction of the church and will warrant extensive information gathering. Perhaps you have some news to share about a construction project or a new member of the leadership team. In that case, you will more than likely need direction and input from your pastor or a staff person. If you have been leading an effort that you are presenting to the congregation, carefully consider how much information your audience needs and cares about. For example, you may have put a tremendous amount of effort and time into getting bids for a project. While the work is important, the congregation probably is not interested in the details of the process. They may just need to know that you received multiple bids. *People do not need a lot of information as much as they need focus.* With the few minutes you have to convey vital information, it is important that you focus on the key message and the actions you think God would have you lead your audience toward.

If your role is to introduce the pastor or speaker, you will need to gather background information, either for the person or for the topic, or both. Be sure to get enough information about the topic to allow you to make an enticing prologue.

If you are welcoming church members, gather information about the service, including the theme for the day or the theme of the message, so you can present an appealing overview. If you are hosting the offering, you may need to find a Scripture that flows with the theme of the day or at least the theme of the message. And if you are the communion host, you will need to gather scriptural background and instruction, along with material from the Bible or another source for your reflection or meditation. Look to someone who has performed a similar role in the past for pointers and strategies for any of these presentation opportunities.

STEP 3 | EXAMPLE

"I get hold of whatever I need to get hold of to gather my content," Chris said. "I get a copy of the worship order from the worship leader to see where my part falls in the service. If it's announcements, I find out what I am supposed to announce and then get all of the details. I think through the announcements and ask myself, 'What is it, how do I need to describe it, who is it for, and what does the person need to do for more information or to get involved?' I ask the questions my audience may ask, and then I think through the answers. If I'm announcing a weekend retreat for couples, I find out if childcare is going to be provided, and then I include the answer in the announcement, even if it is no. I may say, 'There won't be any childcare, so you'll have to arrange for babysitting. But it will be worth it, because it's going to be great!'

"For a communion meditation, I would get my content from the theme for the day and my Scripture meditation. It's great if I can follow the theme for the day, but I'm not tied to it. It's more important to tell something from the heart that helps people focus on Christ."

| STEP 4: MAXIMIZE PREPARATION |

One of the most important aspects of preparing for any presentation is building your confidence by changing the unknown elements into the known. In Chapter 2 of this book, we talk about becoming comfortable with your venue and your equipment. If this is your first time to present in front of the church, go to the room where you will be speaking at a time when the technical team can be there, and walk around on the platform. Stand behind the pulpit. Find out how to coordinate with and cue the technical team on things like slide transitions or music support.

Become familiar with the microphone and speak into it to hear your voice. The key to using all types of microphones is to keep the distance between your mouth and the microphone consistent. Usually the sound technicians can adjust the volume as needed when you keep the microphone about three inches from your mouth. Speakers who are not accustomed to using a microphone often allow it to drift down until it is at chest level or include the mike while making gestures. Another common error is to hold the microphone too close to the mouth. These mistakes make it very difficult for the sound technicians to pick up the speaker's voice or cause them to pick up sounds (such as your breathing) that they can't filter out. If your church uses an "arena" microphone, you don't have to lean into it. A sound check will make sure it's adjusted to the right sensitivity.

Physical transitions often cause some of the most disconcerting unknowns for people who are presenting during a service. Think about how you can keep the transitions tight and eliminate any blank spots or awkward moments. Here are some of the things you will need to consider:

- What is the smoothest and fastest way to get in front of the church? Will you be walking up from the congregation or coming from another area?
- If there is no formal introduction to transition from one element of the service to another, what is your cue?
- If someone does introduce you, will you just take the mike, shake the person's hand, or do something else?
- After your presentation, what will you do with the mike?
- Is it your responsibility to introduce another part of the service? Do you need to give a cue for a smooth transition?

Working physical transitions out with your team ahead of time builds your confidence and allows the service to flow seamlessly and efficiently. Your efforts will make you good stewards of your time! By taking time to pray and think through the various elements in your presentation, being especially mindful of the transitions and jotting your main point and delivery methods down on the 3-D Outline™, you can dramatically affect how people connect with God and each other through the service.

When you are delivering during a worship service, spontaneity is important. The more prepared you are, the more spontaneous you can be. In Chapter 1 we introduced the concept of planned spontaneity. As you spend time completing your 3-D Outline™, looking at the *how* and the *why* of your presentation instead of just the *what*, you will have more confidence. Make a point to know as much as you can about what you are presenting. If you are well prepared, you will be able to relax and focus on the room instead of what you need to say or do next. You'll be able to keep your finger on the pulse of the audience and respond better to what is happening.

If you are well prepared, you will also be able to communicate more efficiently. Brevity is powerful and important. Remember that people think about four times as quickly as you can talk. Therefore, it is important to explain things clearly and to avoid huge leaps in logic that people cannot follow. A simple, powerful statement followed by a pause will often have a much greater impact than a whole paragraph communicating the same idea. With up-front communication, less is almost always more.

Remember that you want to be a good steward of everyone's time. If you have been given two minutes to speak about something and you go over another two minutes, that is twice as long as you were asked to speak. Use every moment to make a powerful impact with the time you have been given.

STEP 4 | EXAMPLE

"When I'm talking about a really short presentation, I like to have it internalized enough so I don't need to refer to my notes," Chris said, "but I always have them in case I blank out. With a little three or four-minute presentation, I will probably just have a few bullet points. In the preparation I really think it through, say it out loud a few times, pray about it, and get comfortable with it so I can be natural."

• Chris makes his physical transitions a little more seamless by wearing a live wireless mike that remains muted until it is time for his part in the service. He turns his mike on and starts talking as he is moving toward the front. "But there are actually certain times in the service when a pause may be great," Chris said, "like at the close of a sermon. People have just been given quite a bit to think about, so that's not necessarily bad dead time. Generally speaking, though, you want to keep those transitions tight."

Here is a possible 3-D Outline™ for making announcements:

3-D OUTLINE™		
Presentation Title:	Announcements	**Del. Date:**
		6/5
Audience:	Congregation	**Start Time:**
		11:10 AM
Objectives:	• Lead people from worship to announcements • Invite involvement in congregational events • Inform congregation of birth announcement • Invite and provide instruction for Guest Registration	**End Time:**
		11:16 AM

Final Preparation Checklist:	[ ] Confirm picnic slides with tech team [ ] Confirm baby picture with tech team		[ ] Review transition with picnic chairperson [ ]	
#	**Time**	**What**	**Why**	**How**	**Who**
1.	30 sec.	Transition from worship	Lead people from worship to announcements	Speaking	Service Host
2.	3 min.	Announce all-church picnic	Invite involvement	Slides, bulletin insert	Picnic Chairperson
3.	1 min.	Announce new small group and introduce leaders	Invite involvement	Speaking	Service Host
4.	30 sec.	Announce birth of Smith baby girl	Inform congregation of birth announcement	Slide (picture)	Service Host
5.	1 min.	Invite guests to register, provide instruction	Invite and provide instruction for guest registration	Speaking, Connect Cards	Service Host
	6 min.	**Total Time**			

A possible outline for the offering might look like this:

3-D OUTLINE™			
Presentation Title:	Receive Offering	**Del. Date:**	
		6/5	
Audience:	Congregation	**Start Time:**	
		11:16 AM	
Objectives:	• Communicate that offering is an act of worship • Offer simple instructions on how to participate • Explain the expectations for participation • Give scriptural support for giving • Receive tithes and offerings for the Lord	**End Time:**	
		11:30 AM	

Final Preparation Checklist:	[ ] Find and meditate on Scripture passage [ ] Connect with the ushers	[ ] [ ]		
#	Time	What	Why	How	Who
---	---	---	---	---	---
1.	30 sec.	Transition from announcements	Lead people from announcements to offering	Speaking	Service Host
2.	30 sec.	Lead congregation to worship experience through offering	Communicate that offering is an act of worship	Speaking	Service Host
3.	1 min.	Give instructions; explain that guests not expected to participate	Offer instructions, explain expectations	Speaking	Service Host
4.	3 min.	Present offering meditation on 1 Chronicles 29:11-14	Give scriptural support for giving	Speaking	Service Host
5.	2 min.	Prayer	Present offering to God	Prayer	Service Host
6.	7 min.	Receive offering	Receive offerings for the Lord	Pass offering baskets	Ushers
	14 min.	**Total Time**			

| STEP 5: OPEN WELL |

Effective verbal transitions from one worship component to the next can tie together the elements of the service to create a cohesive and powerful worship experience. The most significant verbal transition occurs when moving from singing and music to some kind of up-front speaking like communion, the message, and announcements. During these transitions, the audience needs your help to go from one type of experience to the next.

Here are two examples of some simple statements you can use for verbal transitions:

For leading out of teaching into praise and worship: "Wow, I really needed to hear that. When I consider the fact that 'God has plans for us that give us a hope and a future,' I take a lot of comfort in the fact that God knows what he's doing—he's full of love and more merciful than any of us can imagine. Let's use these next few songs to tell him what we think about him."

For leading out of teaching into announcements: "When I am reminded of the transforming power of God, it makes me so glad to be a part of a church where there are so many opportunities to get involved in his work. I want to let you know about a couple of the ways that you can get involved."

Reading a relevant passage of Scripture with passion or inflection is also a great way to help lead people from one experience to the next. But the most appropriate way to help tie the various elements together and to keep God at the center of things is to pray. Ask God to work through the songs, teaching, and other aspects of worship.

You may be leading an element that does not necessarily require a transition—such as the welcome. As simple as it sounds, your best opening is often a simple, "Good morning." You might say something casual and positive, like, "It was beautiful outside this morning, wasn't it?" and follow that with a pause. Then create your own transition into the announcements with something like, "God has really been good to us. Let's be grateful for that as we move into our announcements. I'm so glad it's not raining, because we have our all-church picnic this afternoon." As you glorify God, you are continuing to lead the congregation in worship throughout the announcements.

As you begin, take about ten or twelve seconds to set up your purpose and preview your agenda. For example, you could say, "There are a lot of things going on in our church, but there are four in particular I would like to touch on this morning for just a couple of minutes. And then I'll turn it back over to John."

STEP 5 | EXAMPLE

"For announcements, it's good to open with something really exciting," Chris said. "I may say something like, 'There are some fantastic things going on that I want to tell you about,' or I may tell a joke if it fits the mood of the service. A service host should only use humor if it works for him, his congregation, and the mood of the service. Or I might tie my opening to the message, whatever that was, and the church's core values. Going back to my example about humility, I might say, 'When I think about how important it is to develop this humble spirit, it makes me think about one of our core values, which is servanthood. I want to let you know about a new opportunity to do God's work, which is (whatever the opportunity is).' Or if I just want to keep it generic, I might say, 'Okay, we have sung together, we have taken communion, we have given our offering, and we have had an excellent teaching out of the Bible. We've received a lot today, and now it's time to put it into action. I want to let you know how the church can really be the church Monday through Saturday.' Then I share the announcements."

For the communion meditation, it's great to open with prayer and a simple, crisp, and clear explanation of what is happening. I might say, 'Now we come to that part of the service where we remember what Jesus has done for us, by honoring his body and his blood that the communion elements represent.' Then I might say, 'I would like to share something strange that happened to me earlier this week, which got me thinking about communion.' Then I spend about thirty seconds or so tying an interesting story or anecdote into what communion is all about. It might be good to be totally transparent at times and say something like, 'You know, on Thursday I wasn't even sure I wanted to be a Christian.' Then you might talk about how you are throwing yourself on Christ's grace and go on to talk about the transforming power of his grace."

| STEP 6: ENGAGE YOUR AUDIENCE |

Audio-visual aids are great tools for engaging and connecting with your audience. Use slides, videos, handouts, movie clips, and music that have a strong connection to your presentation as time allows. Handouts and bulletin announcements are excellent interactive tools for this setting. You may want to have the ushers distribute a handout at the beginning of your presentation or include it in the bulletin. Time the distribution of all materials so you don't have to interrupt your presentation or wait for the ushers. If you are covering something that is printed in the bulletin, you may want to ask the audience to look at it as you are speaking and circle or underline something for emphasis. If you are directing the offering, you may ask the ushers to distribute offering envelopes or stewardship cards.

If possible, memorize your presentation so you can use body language, eye contact, and gestures to keep your audience involved. If you need notes, be prepared enough so that you are not tied to them. People listen better when you maintain good eye contact, and they are more likely to receive what you say when they can see your eyes.

When done intentionally, stepping toward a particular section of the room in order to make better contact is an effective communication device. But pacing back and forth can be distracting. Facial expressions—especially a smile—always add to the effectiveness of your message. And physical gestures can communicate passion, humor, and a variety of emotions. As you practice your presentation, adjust your physical gestures to fit the size of the room. As a general rule, the larger the room, the larger the gesture should be.

STEP 6 | EXAMPLE

"Part of engaging your audience really ties into knowing your audience and letting them know that you know they are there," Chris said. "When you say in your prayer, 'There are some here who are having the worst week of their lives,' the person who might be in that place in her life may really perk up to listen.

"I may use a short video or some slides when I am hosting. I usually put the Scripture reference for the communion meditation on the screen. In some churches the person doing communion gives the congregation a few minutes to pray and then talks about the elements and what they represent, then they all take them together. Whatever the church's preference, it is important to give some direction. I might give some direction on what they should be thinking about, like, 'For the next two or three minutes, think about the idea that there is absolutely nothing you can do to be good enough and do for yourself what Christ has done for you. You just have to accept it as a gift.' Then I explain how it's going to happen. ('As the trays come down the aisle, take one of the cups of juice and a piece of bread.') In our church, we give people two or three minutes to pray or meditate before they take the elements of communion, and we may have someone playing softly on the guitar or piano to create some light background sound. I may ask them to pick up the elements and hold them in their hands, and say something like, 'As you feel the bread, I want you to think about the body of Christ that he freely sacrificed.'

"In the announcements, I ask people to take out their bulletins and look at the announcements I am talking about. It's important to ask people to do things to engage and get them involved in what is happening."

| STEP 7: CLOSE WITH ACTION |

In Step 5 we talked about verbal transitions being effective for leading your audience from one worship component to the next. Since a transition leads out of one component into another, it accomplishes its purpose whether it is used as an opening or a closing. Here are two more examples of some simple statements you can use for verbal transitions:

For leading out of the welcome into announcements: "We're really happy that you've connected with us today as we worship God. He's at work all around us, and he uses people who are willing to get involved. We have some ways for you to do that, and John is going to tell you about a couple of them."

For leading out of announcements into the offering: "I hope you've circled in your bulletin these four ways you can worship our awesome God by serving him this week. (List them briefly or remind them of one in particular.) Now we have another opportunity to worship and serve God today as Bill leads us in giving back to God with our offerings."

Probably the most appropriate way to transition out of communion or the offering is to keep God as the focus by praying. Ask God to continue his work through the experience of communion or the offerings given. When you introduce a speaker, ask the congregation to help you welcome the person with applause if your church is comfortable with that. Or you may want to simply turn to the speaker and say, "Thank you for sharing with us today. We're excited to hear what God will be saying through you."

STEP 7 | EXAMPLE

"Where announcements often fall short," Chris said, "is when people don't close with action, like, 'write your e-mail on this form,' or 'make sure you talk to this person after the service.' Or the service host may forget to introduce the person people need to see. You have to be really specific, because there may be people there who have never been to the church before. You can't just say, 'Talk to Andy after the service.' I usually say something like, 'Talk to Andy, our outreach minister. Let me point him out to you. Here's where he is going to be.'"

Whatever your role as service host may be, I pray that this chapter will help you "make the most of every opportunity" (Ephesians 5:16) to lead God's people in a way that honors him.

SCENARIO 2 VIP'S

! When you present to the entire church, you are an important representative of your church to visitors.

! As an up-front communicator, you have the responsibility of *leading* the people in your congregation to take the next step.

! Define the objectives that will drive your words and actions.

! You are not speaking to a crowd, but to a collection of individuals. Think of it as having a conversation with individuals from the front of the church.

! Knowing your audience and understanding its needs are crucial to knowing how to satisfy those needs. Remember that each individual is at a different stage in his or her journey of faith in Christ.

! Brevity is powerful and important. People do not need a lot of information as much as they need focus.

! Keep the physical transitions tight and eliminate any blank spots or awkward moments.

! Effective verbal transitions from one worship component to the next can tie together the elements of the service to create a cohesive and powerful worship experience.

! The more prepared you are, the more spontaneous you can be.

! Memorize your presentation so you can use body language, eye contact, and gestures to keep your audience involved. If you need notes, be prepared enough so that you are not tied to them.

! Facial expressions—especially a smile—always add to the effectiveness of your message.

LEAD AND EMPOWER SMALL GROUPS

> And let us consider how we may spur one another on toward love and good deeds. Let us not give up meeting together, as some are in the habit of doing, but let us encourage one another—and all the more as you see the Day approaching.

—HEBREWS 10:24, 25

Small group ministry has become an essential part of today's church. Small groups often meet in homes for the purpose of spiritual growth, connection, and personal ministry. They have become a crucial vehicle for the church to help its people fulfill their purpose of loving God and loving others, as found in Matthew 22:37. Most church leaders agree that small groups have become a vital component of discipling their members and helping them connect with others.

Regardless of a small group's focus, it is an extension of the church. As such, it should begin with the full support of the church's leadership, and it should champion the vision and goals of the church. While each small group has its own general goals and distinctions, each group will have goals that are unique to its situation and focus. Some groups exist for the purpose of strengthening marriages, while others support and expand upon what is being preached from the pulpit. Other groups reach out to a certain segment of the church or the unchurched population.

Whether a church is small or large, new or established, urban or rural, its small group ministry can serve an important and distinctive purpose. People are usually much more open to one another in small groups. When they are sitting around a table or in a living room with ten or so people, they will gen-erally talk more about the challenges they face and be more receptive to prayer and biblical counsel. They may be encouraged when they hear that others in the group have faced similar challenges. Members draw upon the gifts and talents of others in the group as they live out Hebrews 10:24 by spurring "one another on toward love and good deeds." As people connect together to pray, teach, encourage, grow, and apply biblical truths to their everyday lives, they often forge strong friendships that last for a lifetime. People's lives are changed for the better, group members reach out to help others, and the church better achieves its purpose. In short, successful small group ministries reflect and fuel the church's success in impacting the community.

The many benefits that come from small group ministry can increase ex-ponentially with effective presentation skills. As we apply the *Seven Steps to Effective Presentations* to this ministry scenario, I believe you will see how small group leaders can greatly enhance the discussions and interactions that take place during small group meetings and have a powerful impact on the spiritual growth of their members. Whether you are a full-time leader of the group, are presenting on a rotating basis with other members, or are making a one-time presentation, the good practices and ideas in this chapter will help you achieve greater impact for God's kingdom.

In this chapter we will look at starting and leading an adult small group that meets in a home. Let's look at the seven steps as they apply to small-group ministry.

| STEP 1: CLARIFY OBJECTIVES |

While the overlying objectives for your adult small group will probably be deter-mined in the process of forming the group, there are some general objectives that the leader or the group itself may want to develop. Consider the following:

! What is the basic purpose of the group? For example, is the group going to focus on Bible study, building community, spiritual growth, account-ability, outreach, or a combination of these?
! How often will the group meet?
! Will childcare be provided?
! When will the meeting start and end? Where will it meet?
! Who will be invited and how will you reach the target audience? Does the group have a cap or limit?

! What is the duration or life cycle of the group? For example, is there a defined ending to the group? Does the group have a strategy for multiplication, or will it end on its own?

As the leader of the small group, you will also have specific objectives to set. If you team-teach or rotate teachers, you will need to share and possibly create these objectives with the others so you will all have clarity of purpose. As you develop objectives for individual meetings, consider the following:

! What are the objectives for the particular presentation you are making?
! How will you make people feel comfortable? Will you have a host?
! How do you want people to relate to one another in your group?
! What are your objectives for prayer? Will the members pray for each other's needs or will one person invoke God's blessing and direction?

STEP 1 | EXAMPLE

A friend shared with me that she and her husband lived in a town that had a large military base and a state university. Consequently, many people in their church lived away from home and family and were reluctant to really connect at church because of their transient situation. Others were busy raising teenagers and had not been as involved in the church as they would have liked. My friend and her husband began hosting an adult small group meeting in their home with several objectives in mind:

! Create a sense of community among the small group members
! Encourage connection with and involvement in the church
! Develop close, family-type relationships with the group members

| STEP 2: DEFINE YOUR AUDIENCE |

In this adult small group setting, ask yourself if your members are people who have been part of the group for a while, or will there be people who are new to the church or to the group? As you think through that, remember any objectives you may have set for making new people feel accepted and comfortable. If they have been around for a while, have they connected anywhere else in the church?

Here are some other questions to ask as you define your audience:

! What are some of the likely spiritual and relational needs of your group members?

! Are they married?

! Do they have children?

! Do they have basically the same educational and social background, or will those distinctions vary?

! What is the age range?

! Why are they coming to the group?

STEP 2 | EXAMPLE

The members of my friends' adult small group included single college-age men and women, middle-aged couples with teenage children, and seniors. The group was not defined by age, gender, marital status, or social class. As they had determined prior to starting the group, the common denominator seemed to be the need to belong.

| **STEP 3: GATHER CONTENT** |

There is no end to resources you can use for small group ministry content. Christian publishers and various other Christian organizations have developed complete studies on nearly every topic. You can find studies and resources on books of the Bible, weight loss, Christian stewardship, outreach, and everything in between. You might also use a syllabus provided by the church or choose to develop the study yourself by focusing on a certain passage, subject, or theme. Whatever you use, remember to make sure your material aligns with your church's doctrine, goals, and vision, and find ways to maintain "Bible richness" in your group.

After you have gathered your content, you will need to decide what visual aids you want to use. Handouts, participant books, and teachings on DVDs often serve as effective visuals for small group ministry.

STEP 3 | EXAMPLE

My friend's church had three major components of its mission: people development, creative worship expression, and community impact. To encourage the group's connection with the church, my friend and her husband selected a Bible study curriculum called "Four Great Loves," which was closely aligned with those components. It was an eight-week study that examined practical scriptural direction for loving God, his Word, his people, and his purposes. My friends used the curriculum as the foundation for their group.

| STEP 4: MAXIMIZE PREPARATION |

When you define your objectives for your small group ministry and have clarity about the *whys* related to them, you will be able to prepare with intention and focus. This is the time to use your "strategic thinking" tools that we talked about in Chapter 1. Remember, the strategic (the *why*) drives the tactical (the *how*). Even your seating arrangement is a strategic decision. If your strategy is to create a close-knit feeling, you could put the chairs in a tight circle. If you want to make your members comfortable, use sofas and overstuffed chairs.

Your decision to have a meal before your meeting or to just serve snacks may be driven by the level of interaction you want to take place among your members. Your strategy for interaction may be driven by how well your group knows each other. Meals around a table can allow new people to feel more like part of a family or group, while standing or casual seating for snacks allows your members to circulate, mingle, and get some one-on-one time.

Providing handouts or a writing pad with a pen or pencil may be an outcome of your decision to involve your audience. You may encourage them to take notes or write down questions for a Q&A session at the end of your presentation. You might even give them a short quiz or puzzle that applies to your subject.

It is appropriate for you to maximize your preparation through strategic thinking. However, it is also important to remember that there is a higher strategy that is involved in your small group. As I explained in the introduction to this book, when we are speaking, teaching, or sharing the gospel in any presentation, there is a greater power at work than any human effort we may expend. We do our part when we pray and ask for the inspiration of the Holy Spirit as we prepare, and then we trust that God is at work in both the presenting and receiving of his Word.

Now let's see how the 3-D Outline™ can help you prepare for your small group meeting. If your group has chosen to use a Bible study book, the outline is one piece of the puzzle that you do not need to be concerned about developing. It has been done for you. However, if you are building your own presentation, your 3-D Outline™ will be an indispensable tool for an effective small group meeting. When you break a small group presentation down into the essential segments of the 3-D Outline™, preparation becomes pretty simple. It will help you think strategically, maintain focus, and keep the meeting flowing well. Once you use the outline a few times to help you shape your meeting, you will find it will become an invaluable tool. I have developed the following 3-D Outline™ example for a small group meeting that is focusing on Psalm 103.

3-D OUTLINE™

Presentation Title:	Psalm 103: Jubilant Praise for a Loving God	Del. Date:
		02/09
Audience:	Adult Small Group	Start Time:
		7:00 PM
Objectives:	Overall: • Enhance knowledge and understanding of our loving God Secondary objectives: • Inspire praise • Identify benefits of serving God • Encourage new appreciation for the loving attributes of God	End Time:
		8:00 PM
Final Preparation Checklist:	[ ] Copy handouts [ ] Ask Jim H. to lead opening prayer [ ] E-mail group to think about personal testimonies related to verses 3-7 [ ]	

#	Time	What	Why	How	Who
1.	3	Prayer	Bring correct focus	Individual prayer	Jim H.
2.	3	Read Psalm 103 in NIV	Establish framework	Reading	Susan B.
3.	10	Opening: "Praise the Lord, O my soul"	Inspire praise	Roundtable discussion of vv. 1, 2, biblical examples	Self and Group

#	Time	What	Why	How	Who
4.	15	"Forget not all His Benefits"	Identify Benefits	Handout, discussion of vv. 3-7, personal testimonies	Self and Group
5.	20	The Loving Attributes of God	Encourage appreciation for God	Whiteboard, discussion of vv. 8-19	Self and Group
6.	5	Call to action: Let Praise Dominate Your Life, Psalm 100	Challenge	Speaking, reading, handout	Self and Group
7.	4	Prayer	Praise God	Prayer circle	Group
	60 min. **Total Time**				

Let's say that you and your spouse are leading a small group for married couples, and one of the main objectives for your group is to help the couples revitalize their marriages. So you decide to plan a study on improving communication. Your one-hour presentation might include:

! Opening: 3-4 minutes
! Segment 1: 10 minutes, talking about the biggest communication issues across the board
! Segment 2: 15 minutes, talking about what the Bible specifically says about communication
! Segment 3: 10 minutes, discussing different ideas and facilitating feedback from your audience on some of the best ways they have experienced communication with each other as a couple
! Segment 4: 10-minute quiz with 6 or 8 questions
! Segment 5: 10-minute discussion of responses
! Closing: 5-minute activity of going around the room and asking what group members got out of the discussion and what they will do differently as a result of it

Those bullets could translate into a 3-D Outline™ that looks something like the following.

3-D OUTLINE™

Presentation Title:	Improving Communication with Your Spouse	Del. Date:
		04/19
Audience:	Married Couples Small Group	Start Time:
		7:00 PM
Objectives:	• Gain awareness of communication roadblocks • Reveal biblical truth about communication • Learn good communication practices from others • Rate individual communication awareness	End Time:
		8:00 PM

| Final Preparation Checklist: | [ ] Set up flip chart and markers
[ ] Copy quiz and handouts
[ ] Set out pens and extra Bibles | [ ] Prepare snacks and drinks
[ ] Set out extra chairs
[ ] Turn off cell phone |

#	Time	What	Why	How	Who
1.	3	Opening: Prayer, agenda review	Bring focus	Present	Presenter
2.	10	Major Communication Issues in Marriages	Gain awareness of communication roadblocks	Discussion, flip chart	Group
3.	15	What the Bible Says About Communication	Reveal Biblical truth regarding communication	Scriptures, handout	Presenter
4.	10	Best Communication Practices	Learn good practices from others	Discussion, facilitation	Group
5.	7	Communication Quiz	Rate communication awareness	Quiz	Group
6.	10	Discussion of Quiz Responses	Rate communication awareness	Discussion	Group
7.	5	Closing: Takeaways	Facilitate change in communication practices	Discussion	Group

60 min. **Total Time**

STEP 4 | EXAMPLE

One of my friends' main objectives was to create community and develop close relationships in their small group. So the hosts had a sit-down dinner each week, seating the group members family-style around two tables. They arranged for different members to bring the main course, side dishes, and desserts each week. It seemed that every meal was a hit, and the fellowship around the tables was rich. The hosts used the following setup checklist each week to make sure everything was ready.

SETUP CHECKLIST
Prior to arrival of group
_____ Make coffee
_____ Heat water in teapot
_____ Set out tea bags
_____ Set out canned drinks
_____ Make iced tea (10 tea bags in $3/4$ full large measuring cup, using filtered water; microwave for 10 minutes)
_____ Set out sweetener, sugar, and regular creamer
_____ Set out a napkin and 3 spoons by coffee/hot tea
_____ Set out plates and/or bowls (for 15)
_____ Set out silverware in basket (for 15)
_____ Set out napkins
_____ Set out glasses (for 15)
_____ Set out 6 or 8 cups and saucers
_____ Get ice and put in ice chest
_____ Put scoop in ice chest
_____ Set out salt and pepper (and ketchup or other condiments, if needed)
_____ Set out any food we are preparing
_____ Set out extra chairs at big table
At end of meeting:
_____ Select menu for next meeting
_____ Decide on food assignments

The group sometimes moved to more comfortable seating for the Bible study, but if there were no more than ten people they enjoyed squeezing around the dining room table—it seemed to encourage a more lively discussion. Since they were using a Bible study book, their outline was planned for them. They set out pencils each week so the members could write answers and notes in their books.

SMALL GROUP COVENANTS

Some small groups work together to develop a covenant that clearly defines the expectations for the group. For example, the covenant may list certain disciplines that group members will adhere to, including attendance, confidence, accountability, and responsibility. It could also address the larger issues of purpose and values. The covenant could be a document that the group members agree to sign or simply review and discuss at the first meeting. A sample small group covenant is included in the Resource Section in Part 3 of this book. If you decide to do a covenant, be sure to handle it as a positive reinforcement of the guidelines that will make the group a success.

| STEP 5: OPEN WELL |

Small group ministry is unique in that you actually have several opportunities to create a great first impression. Your first chance may come several days before the meeting when you send out an informational e-mail to your group. You could invite them to the meeting and ask them to think about or read certain things before they get there. A first impression comes when you meet a new couple at church and warmly invite them to join your group. You are making first impressions when you graciously greet people at the door of your home and make them glad they have come. You will make a first impression when you open your mouth to begin your presentation and build good rapport with the group. You should also remember, of course, that those same scenarios present opportunities to create a not-so-great impression.

Remember, people generally make a judgment within the first three minutes. Within moments of reading your e-mail, walking through your door, or listening to your presentation, they will know whether they are excited about being a part of your small group. Put your best foot forward so you do not have to spend the rest of the study catching up.

Look back at the tips I shared in Chapter 1 so you can map out your plan for the opening of your presentation. Connect with your group within the first three minutes so you do not have to spend the next half hour trying to earn buy-in. You already have an advantage—the group members have a vested interest in your success, and they want you to succeed. They are on your side!

In the business world, I have found that there are three things every audience loves: respect (for their time, their dignity, and their feelings), rapport with the speaker, and engagement. I think the same could be said for your small group ministry setting. When Christians get together for fellowship, the camaraderie is usually strong, and it is easy to lose track of time. Be sure to show respect for your group members by starting and ending your presentation on time. In a small group setting, you will most likely know all of your members before starting your presentation, so you already have that one-on-one bond that will carry over into the first three minutes of your presentation. The key to building further rapport with them is to immediately involve them in your presentation.

Look back at the different types of openers we suggested in the first chapter and see which one fits your presentation best. Maybe you will want to start by sharing a short personal experience that relates to your subject or by giving a surprising statistic or bit of trivia. You might want to describe a scene in which your group members can picture themselves. Your opening does not have to be outrageous, just something that is interesting and gets them involved at some level—even if it is only to raise their hands or answer a question. Be sure to not kill your opening by starting with an apology, sharing an unrelated or inappropriate story, or using long and slow-moving statements.

A great way to involve your group from the very beginning is to ask them to define their own expectations. This strategy gets group members involved right away, adds to the rapport, gives members a feeling of ownership, and lets them know you care about their feelings. You could write your group's expectations on a flip chart or writing pad and discuss which ones you can reasonably meet. At the end of your presentation, you can refer back to that list to see how you have met their expectations.

Eye contact builds rapport faster than anything else. In Matthew 6:22, Jesus said that "the eye is the lamp of the body." In other words, the eyes do not lie. Be genuine in what you say, and make solid eye contact with the members of your group. This will create the impression that you are confident and honest and that you care about group members, and it will also keep them alert.

STEP 5 | EXAMPLE

My friends were involved in their welcome team at church, and they were aware of the importance of good first impressions. They made a point to make new people feel welcome and to greet each guest personally as he or she came in. Since fellowship was a high priority around the dinner table, it was often difficult to start the Bible study on time, but they improved in this effort as time went on. She and her husband took turns leading the study, and my friend confessed that her husband actually did a better job of opening the study with an attention-grabbing question, quote, or statistic. But she was quick to add that she was better at connecting with great eye contact.

| STEP 6: ENGAGE YOUR AUDIENCE |

Once you have grabbed your group's attention with your opening, how do you keep them engaged and connected during the body of your presentation, considering that the average adult attention span is only five to seven minutes? You want to ensure that your members will be as fresh and interested at the conclusion as they were the moment your presentation began.

Since we know that people prefer that you talk *with* them instead of *at* them, it's good to engage your group during at least half of your presentation. The best way to engage them is to ask meaningful discussion questions. People who come to small groups are not usually looking for another sermon. They are looking for a chance to dig into the topic and discuss it. Get responses from your extroverts, but be sure to bring in your introverts when you think they may be comfortable sharing a thought or answering a question.

You can also ask your group members to write something down, like filling in the blanks on a handout or writing down your three main points. Foster humor and encourage humorous responses when appropriate. You probably know the names of all of your group members (be sure to use name tags if you don't), so call them by name during your presentation just to let them know they are important to you. Use appropriate stories and anecdotes to create interest and add spice to your presentation.

Don't forget to use the *Strategic Engagement* techniques we talked about in Chapter 4. It is especially easy in a small group setting to engage your audience with fun and interesting activities, games, or skits. Having group members turn and share with a partner helps them really get to know each other, engages them in the presentation, and provides an opportunity to think about their thoughts and feelings before taking the risk of sharing in front of the whole group.

Step 6 | EXAMPLE

Engagement was never a challenge for my friends' group. The Bible study lent itself to discussion through the use of many questions. The diversity of ages and backgrounds in the group made for lively discussion. Those members who were a little shy were encouraged to participate but not pressured. There were some in the group who were quite humorous, so the meetings were always fun. The hosts often used anecdotes and stories to reinforce the point of the lesson, and they sometimes used handouts.

In one of their subsequent studies, they asked one of their group members to lead them in a study on the Feasts of Israel. When they came to the Feast of Purim, the leader decided to make it come to life. The Jewish people initiated the feast to memorialize Esther's heroic act in saving her people from annihilation. The guest speaker led the group in a ceremony that was similar to the ancient celebration. They decorated the room with streamers and balloons as though they were throwing a party. Everyone was given a noise-maker. They brought out the sparkling grape juice. Someone read the story of Esther, and each time the name Haman was mentioned in the story, the people would yell and make noise, stomp their feet, and create all kinds of confusion to stamp out the name of the villain. When the name of Mordecai was mentioned, the people would clap, cheer, and yell. When the name of Esther was mentioned, they would stand and toast her, and then take a drink.

The group thoroughly enjoyed acting out the celebration of the Feast of Purim. Everyone in the room participated and had a great time.

| STEP 7: CLOSE WITH ACTION |

At the end of your presentation, be sure to get feedback from your group members. Ask them for their biggest takeaway or what they are going to do differently as a result of the meeting. You may also want to challenge them by suggesting an action.

Glance back at the 3-D Outline™ example on pages 101-102. The challenge was to let praise dominate your life, and the accompanying praise journal handout facilitated the challenge. Your challenge may be to encourage the group to pray about something, to volunteer, or even to make a change in their lives. You may want to describe how their lives could be different if they were to make such a change. Whatever your challenge, your closing should wrap up the meeting and send your small group members home feeling good about what they learned and inspired to take some kind of action.

STEP 7 | EXAMPLE

My friends shared with me that their group could have done better on this step. They closed with prayer requests and group prayer each week, but they regret that they did not challenge the group with an action or ask for takeaways before the prayer time. My friend explained, "Our group was a huge success, but it could have been even better if we had solidified the study each week with a challenge."

Though the group's objective was to start with dinner at 6:00 and end at 8:00 after Bible study and prayer, most people usually stayed to visit and hang out for a couple more hours. It seemed that no one wanted to go home. Since one of the major objectives that my friends had established was to develop close relationships with these people, they were thrilled with the results. When my friends moved away from that city, they said it really felt like they were leaving family behind.

SMALL GROUPS FOR SINGLES

If you are starting a small group for singles in your church, congratulations! There is a tremendous need for that in churches today. Singleness—especially after college age—is often viewed with suspicion or pity, and singles want neither. They are men and women who want to live rich and full lives. Granted, some are very happy and content in their singleness and others are actively looking for a mate. But in either case, each single should be validated as a whole person with an individual personality and God-given strengths and giftings—especially by the people in his or her church!

As you begin to clarify your objectives for your singles group and define your audience, you will need to sort through several distinctions. (This is actually a time when you will need to combine steps one [Clarify Objectives] and two [Define Your Audience] of the seven-step process.) For example:

! Will it be a mixed group of men and women, or just one or the other?
! Will it include all singles or specific constituents, such as:

- College age?
- Widows and widowers?
- Divorced men and women?
- Single parents with children still at home?

! Will its main purpose be for fellowship and building relationships, or will you have a Bible study or discipleship classes?
! Will you meet once a week, twice a month, or once a month?
! Will outreach be a major objective or an occasional activity, or neither?
! If you have a Bible study, will it be one directed just to singles, or will it be of a more general nature?
! Will "singleness" be an issue that is discussed by the group on a regular basis, or will it be handled on an individual basis?

What are the expectations of the singles in your group? If you are married, what will be your relationship with the group outside of your meeting times? Is it as much a support group as anything, and how much time away from your family are you willing to give?

You may need help sorting through all of these distinctions. Your minister or someone on your church leadership team may be able to help, and be sure to include your spouse if you are married.

Once you have clarified all of your objectives, identify six or eight great resources for your singles—such as Web sites, books, videos, or magazine articles—that answer their questions about singleness, provide encouragement, and offer biblical wisdom and advice. (Check out our Resource Section in Part 3 of this book.) Be sure to update this list often, and refer your singles to these resources when they need uplifting or have questions you cannot answer.

If your meetings will be for Bible study or discipleship, you will need to decide on a curriculum (Step 3, Gather Your Content). You may want to make this a group decision. Do they want to:

! Have a Bible study, using a pre-prepared study guide?
! Study a specific book of the Bible or a Bible-related topic?
! Explore the topic of Christian singleness?
! Study a discipleship-type book, like *Wild at Heart* (for men) by John El-dredge, or *Living a Life of Balance: Women of Faith Study Guide Series*.

For steps four through seven, refer back to Chapters 3 and 4 of this book to help you prepare your presentations and have engaging meetings.

You have a great opportunity to make a difference in the lives of the singles in your group. God bless you!

SCENARIO 3 VIP'S

! A small group should begin with the full support of the church's leadership and should champion the vision and goals of the church and its denomination.

! While the overlying objectives for your small group will probably be determined in the process of forming the group, there are some general objectives that the leader or the group itself may want to develop.

! Make sure your ministry material aligns with your church's doctrine, goals, and vision, and be sure to maintain "Bible richness" in your group.

! Handouts, participant books, and teachings on DVDs often serve as effective visuals for small group ministry.

! Use strategic thinking and allow your objectives to drive such decisions as seating arrangements and whether to serve a meal around a table or to serve snacks in a casual setting.

! Using a 3-D Outline™ to prepare for your small group ministry will help you think strategically, maintain focus, and keep the meeting flowing well.

! Be sure to show respect for your group members by starting and ending your presentation on time.

! The best way to engage your small group audience is to ask meaningful discussion questions.

MAXIMIZE TEACHING OPPORTUNITIES

> Therefore go and make disciples of all nations, baptizing them in the name of the Father and of the Son and of the Holy Spirit, and teaching them to obey everything I have commanded you. And surely I am with you always, to the very end of the age.

—MATTHEW 28:19, 20

Teaching the Word of God is both a tremendous privilege and a great responsibility. Whether you are teaching in a Sunday school class, a Bible study group, a vacation Bible school, or a special workshop, you have the awesome opportunity, with the Holy Spirit working through you, to transform lives. You are a co-laborer with Jesus Christ, who decreed in Matthew 28:19, 20 that we are to make disciples, baptize them, and then teach them his Word. Effective teaching equips and empowers Christians. It deepens their understanding of God's Word and helps them to live by its teachings.

There are many different teaching opportunities within the church, but Sunday school is likely the most prevalent. Sunday school impacts all ages in the church. In Sunday school future leaders are trained, people form strong and meaningful relationships, and the foundation of faith is laid and strengthened over a lifetime. We will use Sunday school as our model in this chapter as we look at the presentation techniques that will help you become an effective "life transformer."

I believe that incorporating the skills I share in this chapter will help you bring added value to your students and impact their lives in a greater way.

It is important for Sunday school teachers to grow in their own walks with the Lord, pray for wisdom, and pursue knowledge and skills that will help them be as effective as possible. Before we start through the *Seven Steps to Effective Presentations*, I encourage you to think through your situation as a Sunday school teacher so you can get the big picture. This perspective will give you more clarity about the things you need to do to optimize your role as you go through the seven steps.

There are three things to look at as you are considering the big picture: your role, the philosophies under which you will be operating, and your environment. Are you the primary teacher, a helper, or a substitute teacher? You may be in a larger church where you are the primary teacher but you have several helpers. How long have you committed to your role? Perhaps you have committed to being involved on an ongoing basis.

What philosophies and expectations are associated with your role? If you are filling in as a substitute teacher, make sure you are in alignment with the tone and direction that have been established for the class. If possible, talk to the primary teacher and find out his or her objectives for the class, as well as the expectations. Then you can plan your lessons to meet or exceed those expectations.

If you have taken over the responsibility for the overall management and teaching of a class, begin by discerning what God would have you do with the class. Then you will need to make sure you know what the church leadership wants you to do with that responsibility. How does your class curriculum fit in with the overall education objectives of the church? with the mission of the church? with the mission of the department or the particular age group within the department? If you are in a smaller church or a church that is just beginning, these distinctions may not be clear, and that is okay. You can usually get clarity from your pastor or someone else on your church's leadership team. If that is not an option, just move ahead based on what you believe God is leading you to do.

The last frame in the big picture is your environment. What type of facility will you be using, and do you have a choice in that decision? Does it change from time to time? Do you share a large room divided by folding partitions, or are you in a traditional classroom? Maybe your class meets in one corner of the sanctuary. Your environment will have a big impact on your presentation methods and strategies. It influences the types of visuals you use as well as the type of interaction you have with your audience.

Once you have clarity on your role, your philosophy, and your environment, you can see how your class fits into the bigger picture of the ministry of the church. Now let's look at the *Seven Steps to Effective Presentations*, which will help you bring even more value to your role as a Sunday school teacher.

Since Sunday school covers such a wide variety of ages, with each age group requiring vastly different presentation techniques, I have divided the remaining part of the chapter into three segments. I will address the age distinctions by going through the *Seven Steps to Effective Presentations* for young children, teens, and adults. I have zeroed in on the ideas that apply specifically to the three groups so you can go directly to the one that applies to your particular situation, or you may want to read all three segments to get a clear view of the overall picture.

YOUNG CHILDREN | STEP 1: CLARIFY OBJECTIVES |

What better opportunity to help parents frame and shape a child's relationship with God than to teach that child at an early age in Sunday school? We have probably all heard adults affectionately refer to Sunday school teachers who had a great impact on their lives. So one of your objectives may be to build a strong, supportive relationship with each child and his or her parents. I encourage you to make praying for your students and their salvation another objective that is high on your list.

My daughter Paige was in the fifth grade when she was baptized. She had gone to the same Christian school for all five years, and all five of her teachers had been praying for her salvation the entire time. Four out of the five teachers took the time to attend her baptismal service on a Sunday afternoon, and the fifth would have been there if a family situation had not preempted it! Their presence had a huge impact on Paige and was a great encouragement in her Christian walk. Consider having that kind of prayer involvement and relationship with your students.

Actively involving parents in their child's spiritual development, when feasible, is another great objective. There is only so much you can do when you have the child one hour of the week. If the parents are willing, they can continue your teaching with different activities during the week and reinforce the truths the child learned on Sunday. Consider sending a note home with the children asking for the parents' help and encouraging them to fulfill their God-given responsibility, as found in Deuteronomy 6:6, 7: "These commandments that I give you today are to be upon your hearts. Impress them on your children. Talk about them when you sit at home and when you walk along the road, when you lie down and when you get up."

Since some of the parents may not attend church, another great objective may be to reach out to the children's families and friends by cascading the Sunday school message to them each week. Children generally share proudly and enthusiastically when they have something to show. Sending them home with a handout, a picture they have drawn or colored, or a craft they have made will enable them to share with their families what they learned in Sunday school. It will also reinforce the lesson to the children each time they tell it.

Additional objectives may include helping children grow in their understanding and knowledge of God and helping them come to an understanding of who Jesus is. Another may be to enhance learning by using engaging learning methods. Some of your sub-objectives may include helping the children learn to cooperate and learn consideration of others, teaching them to make good choices, and helping them learn responsibility. Your presentation objectives will likely change with every lesson you teach.

STEP 1 | EXAMPLE

Monica is the children's minister at a medium-sized church in the northeast. She shared that her children's Sunday school department has three primary objectives. They teach their children:

! That church is a happy place.
! That the Bible is a special book.
! That Jesus wants to be their friend.

Monica read Denise Oliveri's article that we have included in this chapter, "What Makes a Good Sunday School Teacher?" and she offered an additional requirement: To have a growing relationship with Jesus. "No one can lead where they have not been," she said.

| STEP 2: DEFINE YOUR AUDIENCE |

The age range of the children you will be teaching is the most important consideration in defining your audience. Children experience tremendous changes in their developmental and cognitive abilities in relatively short periods of time. The size of your class and teacher-to-student ratio will determine how you manage your teaching. With a larger class, you will likely need to think about how you will include and manage helpers. You may need to build in time and transition strategies to move from opening activities, like a Bible story or a puppet show, to smaller discussion groups.

Consider your audience's background, frame of reference, and attention span. There may be some in your class who were not brought up attending church and know nothing of the Bible, while others have heard the Bible stories all of their lives. Children with emotional or behavioral challenges or disabilities can have a dramatic effect on your classroom. Think about how you will help these children successfully learn without disrupting your class. All of these factors will affect how you plan and deliver your lesson.

STEP 2 | EXAMPLE

Monica attends a multi-site church. As the children's minister over all of the sites, she ensures that their children's Sunday school classes cover no more than a two-year span, but she allows the directors in each church to decide how to make that split. The ages range from birth to sixth grade, and the directors adjust their classes based on how many attend their Sunday school in each range. "Jesus did not dictate what age group to have in a class," she explained. "You don't want to create a class that has no one in it." How the directors split the classes depends on teacher availability and what students they have, keeping in mind the developmental differences in each age. The teachers base their teaching techniques on such distinctions as socio-economic differences and whether their students are highly churched or not.

| STEP 3: GATHER CONTENT |

Your church's children's ministry structure will determine how you gather your content for your teaching. Many churches provide curriculum or books that spell out the lessons for each week. Sometimes the content will be left up to you. Obviously, you will want to start with the Bible. But to effectively reach your audience, it's important to include interactive and age-appropriate activities and experiences, such as Standard Publishing's

HeartShaper curriculum for children's ministry or Steven James's *Sharable Parables*. You can find a wealth of materials at your local Christian bookstore or at Internet sites like www.standardpub.com, kidssundayschool.com and Christiancrafters.com. Check with your children's ministry director to see what resources are available. Respect and support your leader's plan for Christian education. If you find materials that you feel are especially effective, ask your leader for his or her opinion on using them.

Since this age group requires you to use many different delivery methods, your content may actually come from several different sources. You may start with the Bible story from the lesson book provided by your church, for example, and then pull things from the Internet or other sources to supplement the basic lesson. Most leaders involved with children's ministry welcome creativity in the classroom. So use your imagination to build on the lessons you have been given.

In my experience with various groups of children over the years, I have used a number of different activities. With one group, I decided to do a scavenger hunt to teach the concept of discovery. As I was gathering my content, I went on the Internet and did a search under the keywords "scavenger hunt." I looked at several of the different scenarios that came up and pulled one or two items from each. I then combined them into a list of about fifteen items for the hunt. I divided the kids into teams and gave each team an inexpensive instant camera so they could take pictures of the items they found. They brought the pictures back and we put them on a flip chart. It was a fun activity, and it really brought home the excitement of discovery for the children.

STEP 3 | EXAMPLE

Monica recommends that teachers of young children use pre-printed curriculum. "It is difficult to replicate the scope and sequence that professional publishing houses have included in their curriculum," she said. "Every curriculum has its strengths and weaknesses, but it is usually better to have a pre-written curriculum and work with it than to try to develop your own. Very little individually written curriculum has the breadth that published curriculum has. It is very time-consuming to write your own, and you want to make the best use of your teacher's time. It's often better to use that time in building relationships."

| STEP 4: MAXIMIZE PREPARATION |

When a teacher relies completely on the curriculum or fails to really absorb and understand the prepared lesson, he is really shortchanging himself and the kids. Remember that we are delivering the most important message a child will ever hear. It is worth our full effort and attention. Begin working on your lesson early in the week. Waiting until Saturday night to prepare puts undue pressure on you, stifles your creativity, and does not allow you adequate time to think and pray about what God wants to say through you.

I want to encourage you to use the 3-D Outline™ to help you prepare—even if you don't use all of the columns. Completing the time element and the *what* and *how* columns will help you plan and visualize the entire session. As you plan each segment of your Sunday school time, think of the average attention span for your age group. You will want to move fairly quickly from one activity to another when you are teaching young children, so you may end up with five or six segments. But remember that younger children actually learn more if you stick to the same routine each week. Be sure to provide some playtime at the end for that age group to make it fun for them and make them want to come back.

There are usually latecomers in any Sunday school class, so you may want to plan a light activity for the first few minutes so everyone can start the lesson together. You can also use this time to get to know the children or ask them about things that are going on in their lives. You may want to spend the next fifteen minutes presenting the Bible lesson to the entire group. If the size of your class warrants it, break out into smaller groups for some kind of activity. If space is an obstacle, you may consider setting chairs in a circle for your breakout groups. If time, weather, and circumstances allow, you may even want to conduct some of your activities outside or in a hallway or larger room. Just be sure you have enough supervision to make this a safe activity and that you understand your children's ministry safety guidelines.

I have found that blue painter's masking tape is a great tool for any age group for making circles or lines on the floor to indicate where people should gather or stand for an activity. Kids love it because of its bright color, and it's a fun way to direct them where to go for the next step. It works great on either carpet or tile and is easy to remove.

After your activity, you may want to bring the group back together for a time of worship and then close with prayer. It would be good if you can have some of the children pray or at least participate in part of the prayer.

The *how* part of your outline, or your method of delivery, is especially important for children. Will you be using a handout, an activity sheet, a skit or a video, dress-up clothes, puppets, a movie clip, or crafts? In the "Final Preparation Checklist" section near the top of the form, remember to list the gathering of toys, props, videos, music CDs, or anything else you may need in your teaching session.

Let's look at a possible 3-D Outline™ for a lesson like we have just described:

3-D OUTLINE™

Presentation Title:	A Wife for Isaac		Del. Date:
			06/10
Audience:	Sunday School Class, Ages 5 and 6		Start Time:
			9:30 AM
Objectives:	• Demonstrate Abraham's Faith • Show God's Faithfulness • Demonstrate that God Answers Prayer		End Time:
			10:30 AM
Final Preparation Checklist:	[ ] Set up puppets and action figures [ ] Prepare craft materials	[ ] Put blue painter's masking tape on floor [ ] Bring worship CDs	

#	Time	What	Why	How	Who
1.	10	Play time, visit with kids	Settle in, build relationships	Toys, talking	Teachers, children
2.	15	Bible lesson: A Wife for Isaac	Demonstrate: Abraham's faith, God's faithfulness, God answers prayer	Puppets, action figures	Primary teacher
3.	15	Break-out activity	Reinforce lesson	Craft	Helpers
4.	10	Worship	Teach worship, reinforce lesson	Music CD	Teachers, children
5.	10	Closing: Review lesson, cascade lesson	Reinforce lesson, reach families	Questions, review take-home items	Primary teacher
	60 min.	**Total Time**			

STEP 4 | EXAMPLE

"No teacher can do her job efficiently without adequate preparation," Monica said, "even if using good curriculum. Of course a lesson goes better when a teacher has worked on it all week. They can be creative, add their own touches, find special supplies, etc. But since fewer teachers really have the time and energy to do that type of prep these days, we try to compensate by using curriculum that does not require tons of preparation to teach well and by providing a well stocked supply room that teachers know they can count on. We also use teaching teams wherever possible so that the scope of what one teacher is responsible for is manageable."

| STEP 5: OPEN WELL |

It is a great idea to greet children as they come through the door and to visit with them for a moment as you are waiting for others. When you start the lesson, get children excited about what they will be doing so they will look forward to the experience. You might even introduce the story with a teaser like, "We're going to find out today why a man named Jonah ended up inside the belly of a very big fish!" After the opening prayer, you might start with an energetic song to get things going. You can introduce the story with a quick creative device like putting a fish net over your head or shoulders, complete with seaweed!

STEP 5 | EXAMPLE

Monica shared that their teachers' first goal of the morning is to make each child feel welcomed and get settled in. They train their teachers to keep their eyes on the door and watch for the children to arrive. They want every child to be noticed and then invited to engage. They start the children off playing with toys, puzzles, or games, and then they move to one or two activities that point toward the teaching theme.

| STEP 6: ENGAGE YOUR AUDIENCE |

Toys and props make great tools for helping younger children connect with the Bible story. "Talking" stuffed animals and puppets have a big impact on younger children and help them remember the story. Using these tools allows you to relate information at their level, encourages the children to participate, and even gives them the courage to talk in front of the other kids. When I once was asked to teach a class of young children, I bought an inexpensive plastic toy microphone and had the kids talk into it to answer the questions I asked. Even the shy ones loved it! They grabbed the microphone and belted out their answers!

Singing is a great way to engage the kids, and the younger ones especially enjoy using hand and body gestures. Be sure to tie everything together—the lesson, all of the songs, and each activity, game, and craft—to the main point and objectives of the lesson.

If you're teaching fourth through sixth grade, you may want to include real-life stories, Bible dictionaries and maps, props, videos, or movie clips. This age group may enjoy acting out the story or having contests like Bible drills. Games and arts and crafts also work well for this age. Use humor where appropriate, and you may want to reward children for attendance and Scripture memorization.

STEP 6 | EXAMPLE

Monica says that children respond to routine. She advises teachers not to do the same activities every week, but to create a pattern of activities. Her teachers usually do an opening activity that introduces the topic with some sort of interaction (a game or some kind of art or drama experience). Then they tell the Bible story with a scriptural truth and conclude with an application activity. She says they are considerate of most kids' learning stages and keep in mind the three different learning styles (auditory, visual, and kinesthetic, or hands-on). Over a period of a quarter, they make sure they incorporate activities that appeal to each style.

| STEP 7: CLOSE WITH ACTION |

In step one, Clarify Objectives, we talked about the importance of sending something home with the children that will both cascade the message of the lesson to their family members and remind the children of the point of the lesson each time they see it. As you close, be sure to reinforce those objectives by reminding the children to share an object, such as a handout, a craft, or a Bible verse printed on a 3x5 card, with their families or caretakers. You may even want to ask one or two of the children what the object represents and let them retell the story for the class. This will also model what all the kids could tell their families. You might even take it one step further and encourage them to talk to two people about Jesus that week or invite someone to church. Tying the object you are sending home to an action like this dramatically increases the chances that kids will follow up.

Don't underestimate the impact a motivated child can have. A friend told me a story recently involving her three-year-old granddaughter, Kelsey. Kelsey's Sunday school teacher had been talking to the children about telling others about Jesus. She did not quite understand the concept, so she asked her mother how to do that. Her mother explained that when you are visiting with someone, you might just talk about Jesus and what he has done in your life.

Kelsey and her mother were at her pediatrician's office a few days later, and Kelsey found a little playmate about her age in the waiting room. Kelsey's new friend was called to the back for her appointment. When she came back out, Kelsey and her mother were still in the waiting room. There was a glass partition separating them since the little girl was on her way out. Telling the little girl about Jesus had apparently been on Kelsey's mind the whole time. When she saw her new friend on the other side of

WHAT MAKES A GOOD CHILDREN'S SUNDAY SCHOOL TEACHER?

Denise Oliveri, owner of the Pre-school Sunday School Central Web site, says that to be a great Sunday school teacher, "you don't have to know the Bible inside and out, and you don't have to be an expert in religion. You can be a great Sunday school teacher by doing what you enjoy doing most—having fun with kids."[6] In her article entitled "What Makes a Good Sunday School Teacher?" that appeared on the idea-marketers.com Web site, Denise says a great Sunday school teacher will:

! Have a passion. Good Sunday school teachers love teaching and spending time with kids.

! Love kids. Kids seem to know people who really enjoy kids, and they are drawn to those people.

! Make a commitment. As a Sunday school teacher, you will be asked to plan and carry out regular lessons and teach your class each and every Sunday. If you cannot commit to a weekly class, then you may be better off helping instead of teaching.

! Stay organized. You will need to take the time to organize your lessons and find the materials you will need when you teach. Even if you don't feel comfortable making lesson plans, you can find great info in books and online that will help you.

! Have fun. If you have fun and you enjoy what you are doing each week, the kids will have fun, too. You will be a success.

the glass partition, Kelsey put her hand on the glass to get her attention and mouthed the word, "Jesus."

STEP 7 | EXAMPLE

Monica's teachers always send something home with the children that tells the parents what they did and gives them some ideas for helping the kids apply the lesson during the week. "The bottom line is I want kids to go home with a concrete idea of how the lesson they just learned from the Bible about God, about themselves, or about his kingdom will translate into their everyday lives. If they learn that God kept his promise to Noah, that is only the beginning. They must also understand that God is a promise keeper. God keeps his promises to them as well." They might ask the children, "What promises has God made you? Why is that special or important? How does it help you trust in that truth this week?" "If we have not caused them to think or act differently, then we have not done our jobs," she said. "We discern that by using an application activity and send home a memory jogger. The application activities may include talking about how the lesson applies to their lives, praying, playing a game that relates to the lesson, writing an action plan, making a visual reminder, acting out some real-life scenarios, or any number of other things."

TEENS | STEP 1: CLARIFY OBJECTIVES |

By the time kids reach middle school, their decision to attend church and which church to attend is often influenced dramatically by their peers. One objective as a Sunday school teacher is to find ways to make your class time so enjoyable and meaningful for them that they will want to come back week after week with their friends. Of course, you will also want to help them deepen their walk with the Lord in the process. That is no small feat, indeed!

Since we are including both teens and preteens in this section, your objectives will obviously need to address the different age groups. Your church may combine the Sunday school classes for middle school and high school, or bring them together for the opening Bible lesson and then separate them out by age. Or you may have separate classes for the different age groups. You may be a primary teacher for a combined class, or you may be a helper in a senior high class. Whatever your role, you will need to establish your objectives within the parameters of your role, as we discussed at the beginning of the chapter.

As with the younger children, one of your objectives with the teens may be to build a strong, supportive relationship with each of them. At this age, kids often need someone other than their peers or their parents who will listen and be there for them through all of their ups and downs. That person should help steer them in the right direction in the process. When teens at your church see that you are someone they can trust, do not be surprised if they seek you out for counsel.

One objective remains the same no matter what age group you are teaching—helping your audience grow in its knowledge and understanding of the Lord. As a response to Matthew 28:19, 20, you should be ready to lead students who do not know him to the Lord. Of course, you will also have weekly objectives that you will want to accomplish with each of your lessons, but these should flow with your overall objectives.

STEP 1 | EXAMPLE

Kassie attends a large church in Texas, and for two years she taught teenage girls, ages thirteen to eighteen. The girls called themselves the Army Girls, and Kassie identified their objectives like this:

1. She wanted to equip them to be soldiers for God, to be mighty in spirit, strong in the Lord, and effective in engaging in the warfare of the Christian life.

2. She wanted the girls to focus on their identity in Christ and as a daughter of God, understanding that other things may change, but their identity never will.

| STEP 2: DEFINE YOUR AUDIENCE |

There is a world of difference between a seventh grader and a senior in high school. As you teach teens, consider both their age and their maturity level. Middle school kids have just begun to engage in abstract thought. High schools kids are still exploring it. Physiological and social pressures and influences are forcing dramatic change and serious questions for teens. Prayerfully consider the maturity level of the kids in your class or group. It's important to meet the kids right where they are.

Consider the background of the teens in your class. Are there different socio-economic groups represented? If so, that may bring up a whole new set of challenges and objectives. Are they all in the same school district, or do they go to competing schools?

What are their interests? In an article on the *ehow.com* Web site called, "How to Teach a Teen Sunday School Class," Kathleen Fuller wrote, "Give your students an interest inventory on the first day of class. . . . Include questions such as 'What is your favorite way to spend your free time?' 'How often do you read the Bible?' 'What kind of music do you like?' Understanding your students' interests can help you plan an effective lesson."[7] If you have contact information, you may want to do this prior to the first class so you can get more clarity on your objectives.

STEP 2: | EXAMPLE

Kassie's audience was a little unique for a teen class. This was a special class of teenage girls that began as a result of several parents coming to Kassie and asking that she disciple their daughters. They were from the same socio-economic class. Some were home-schooled and some attended private schools. These girls were all Christians and all came from families who loved the Lord and had a heart to grow spiritually. They had all received good, solid spiritual training at home and knew that they wanted to own their own faith and grow in it.

| STEP 3: GATHER CONTENT |

If curriculum for youth ministry is not provided by your church, you can find one at a Christian bookstore or on the Internet. Doug Field's *Simply Youth Ministry* at *www.simplyyouthministry.com* has tremendous youth curriculum. Standard Publishing's Encounter™ curriculum is also highly effective. You can, of course, develop your own. As you do, remember that teens are no longer kids, but neither are they ready to be taught as adults.

This is where you really want to get creative and come up with interesting ways to get the gospel across. It's important to remember, however, that entertainment and social activities for teens are secondary to teaching the gospel. Teen ministry must be grounded in sound Bible doctrine, or it loses its relevancy to the mission of the church. You want to filter in the teens' expectations and interests, but not at the expense of biblical integrity or alignment with the mission of your church and denomination. It is also important for you to remember to just be who you are. You don't have to pretend to be cool or relevant if you are not. Teens will see through the charade in the first thirty seconds anyway.

There are many resources that provide excellent multiple learning activities for teens to supplement your lessons. *Rbpstudentministries.org* is a great source for teen curriculum, and Standard Publishing (*standardpub.com*) has some incredible digital Bible lessons that address real-life issues for teens. Their Web site describes them as lessons that "empower students to interact first-hand with the Bible and learn how God helps with the struggles they face every day."

You can also ask the teens in your group to help gather content. Teens are usually more than happy to help you find a video clip, song, story, or image that works with your lesson. If you enlist the help of your teens, make certain you preview the content before you show it. You might also want to dig into the content's source, as using it as part of your presentation is an implied endorsement of the artist or source.

STEP 3 | EXAMPLE

Kassie developed her own content. She started with a lot of prayer. "I would really pray, and God would give me a passage to focus on," she said. "I also studied the girls to see what their needs were. It helped that I had been a teenage girl not that long ago myself. I asked myself, 'What were the things I was facing? What were my challenges and struggles? What were the areas I knew I could have used more wisdom in?' Then I took that before God and prayed about it. I said to him, 'Here's the need. How can we best meet that need?'"

"We studied different passages of Scripture over several weeks," Kassie said. "One was 2 Peter 1:5-7, where it talks about different character traits we as Christians need to develop. I covered one character trait a week. I did a word study on each topic, using cross-references in the Bible, *Vines Expository Dictionary of the Old and New Testaments, Webster's Dictionary*, and any other sources I could find. I did Google searches just to see what was out there. I also sought wise counsel from my parents, who have been involved in ministry for a long time, and from my sister, who had taught a girls' Bible study."

| STEP 4: MAXIMIZE PREPARATION |

It is very important to start working on your lesson early in the week for all age levels. That is especially true with this age group, since teens often interpret lack of preparation as lack of caring. Waiting until Saturday night to prepare for your teen Sunday school class limits your options for creativity. And since teens have so many thoughts and issues going on in their lives, you certainly do not want to wait until the last minute to pray about what God wants you to say.

Unless you are using a pre-planned Bible lesson or curriculum, I would encourage you to use the 3-D Outline™ to plan your lesson. In the space provided at the top, list the objectives you have established for this particular lesson, and then envision the activities that will help you reach those objectives. You might want to start with an icebreaker that would introduce the lesson and get the teens involved. I mentioned in the children's ministry section of this chapter that I had orchestrated a scavenger hunt for a group of young children. You could do a personal or spiritual scavenger hunt for teens that has them looking for people in their group or biblical characters with certain personality or spiritual traits.

Make sure your Bible lesson ties to something that teens deal with on a regular basis, like anger, worry, choices, or courage. Be sure to build in time for discussion. If allowed to express themselves, teens will usually get much more out of the lesson. You can round off your session with a game or some kind of activity that reinforces your lesson.

A 3-D Outline™ for a teen Bible study lesson may look something like this:

3-D OUTLINE™

Presentation Title:	Friendship			Del. Date: 06/12
Audience:	Teen Girls (Ages 13–14)			Start Time: 9:30 AM
Objectives:	• Identify Qualities of a Good Friend • Gain Biblical Grounding re Friendship • Facilitate Commitment to Better Friendships			End Time: 10:30 AM
Final Preparation Checklist:	[ ] Set up flip chart and markers			

#	Time	What	Why	How	Who
1.	5	Opening • Prayer • Reveal Topic	Set Tone	Prayer, discussion	Teacher
2.	10	Question: What Makes a Good Friend?	Involvement, identify qualities of a good friend	Facilitate, write answers on flip chart	Teacher, class
3.	20	What Does the Bible Say About Friendship?	Gain biblical grounding re friendship	Small group activity (groups of 3)	Class
4.	20	Report Out from Groups	Engagement	Rotation report-outs and group discussion	Teacher, class
5.	5	Action to Take: How I Will Serve God by Being a Good Friend	Facilitate commitment to better friendships	Each participant shares what she will do differently	Class/ teacher
	60 min.	**Total Time**			

STEP 4 | EXAMPLE

"I started preparing early each week," Kassie said. "When I developed the curriculum, I made an outline that included each week's lesson, so I knew what I would be talking about each week.

"I know that engaging your audience is really effective, especially for this age group, so it was my goal to have one engaging activity each week. We did games, crafts, skits, videos, or something that I knew would be meaningful for the girls. One week we did a clue hunt, similar to a scavenger hunt. I planted clues all around the room and they had to track them down. The final clue was hidden in the Bible, which illustrated my point about seeking truth in the Word of God.

"I continually involved the parents, talking with them every few weeks about what the girls were learning and getting input from them about the girls' needs."

GOOD BIBLE STUDY FOR CHRISTIAN TEENS

In her article "Tips for Running a Good Bible Study for Teens," Kelli Mahoney has some obvious and not so obvious suggestions for how to help your time spent in a teen Bible study go well. First in the obvious category is to provide food. While it doesn't have to be a meal, soda and chips are essentials. Also, set up the room ahead of time to provide a comfortable place for kids to hang out. Then, because teens can be forgetful even about essentials, have plenty of extra Bibles and student books available. That way you're ready for any guests that might show up.

Some less obvious tips include having an agenda. While teens like variety, they also want to be able to know what to expect. An agenda keeps things from going too far off-track. Balancing out the agenda idea is the tip to "be flexible." Because things don't always go as planned and deep discussions can arise unexpectedly, learn to go with the flow and allow God to guide the Bible study in the direction he sees fit.

Her last tip is obvious but not always practiced: pray. Seek God's help before each Bible study so that you can be the best leader possible. Also plan prayer times in which your students can participate and grow spiritually.[8]

| STEP 5: OPEN WELL |

When teenagers walk into your Sunday school room, they are going to be looking for something that will hold their interest. If it is their first time in your class, they will probably be wondering if it will be worth their time or if they will fit in. So get their attention and make them feel comfortable right off the bat, perhaps with an icebreaker or an opening question. Make sure, of course, that the question provides a good lead-in to your lesson. You want the opening activity or question to foreshadow where you are going so it will pique the kids' interest.

STEP 5 | EXAMPLE

Kassie said, "My opening was different each week. I sometimes used ice-breakers or riddles. One week I made little cards with words on them and handed them out to the girls. They played charades, acting out the words on the cards. Afterwards, I spread the words out on the table and gave them three minutes to tell me how they were all related. They were all words describing what love was or was not, from the Scripture passage we had been studying, 1 Corinthians 13.

"For the last quarter, I asked one girl each week to open the lesson for me. We called this our 'Happy Girls Opening.' I would tell the girl who was assigned for the next week what I would be doing for the lesson that week. Then I gave her the freedom to do whatever she wanted. With their unique personalities, they each did something different and wonderful. It was really amazing! One girl had just returned from China when it was her turn to open. She did a great presentation about the ministry opportunities she had in China and had handouts written in Chinese! When the girls opened, they quickly realized how important it was to have an appreciative audience that was really engaging, so they became more attentive to the lessons and more appreciative of what they were learning."

IDEAS TO ENGAGE KIDS

For some great activities for vacation Bible school, check out an article by Kimberly L. Keith on about.com titled "Ideas for Vacation Bible School." One activity that she suggests is a Bible baseball tournament with two teams answering questions in order to advance around the bases. For each at bat a child is asked four questions (based on the VBS lessons) until he or she comes up with a correct answer. The hardest question (homerun) is asked first and the easiest question (first base), last. Consider using it on the final day of VBS to review all the Bible information students learned during the week. Another activity that the author found surprisingly successful was having a group of fourth-grade boys spend a week making an old-fashioned salt map of the Holy Land. [9]

Another excellent VBS tip comes from Amity Alicea's blog on the *http://ministry-to-children.com/vacation-bible-school-tips* Web site: "We had difficulty finding skit actors this year, so our youth group is taking on the project of creating and videotaping the skits that will be shown each night. This gives the high-school age kids an opportunity to get involved and serve, as well as meeting a need and solving a problem."

STEP 6: ENGAGE YOUR AUDIENCE

This step is important with all Sunday school ages, but it is absolutely critical with teens. Remember, many teens are dealing with peer pressure about going to church. So it is important that they have an interesting and enjoyable experience.

Once you grab them with your opening activity or question, keep them involved. Look for creative ways to get teens to participate in the delivery as well as the learning. You may even want to have some of the teens present the Bible lesson or report back on an assignment you gave the week before. You could ask them to journal their devotions with the Lord one week, and then have them share something that challenged them.

You might also want to form subgroups for about ten minutes, have the teens look up something in the Bible, and then come back together for a discussion. In your Bible lesson and discussion times, open-ended questions work well with most teens once they have a level of comfort with the group.

STEP 6: | EXAMPLE

"The girls loved doing skits, so we did several," Kassie told me. "One of my favorites was one we did on spiritual warfare. We had been studying about how the enemy can come in and gain ground suddenly if we're not guarding our hearts. We learned that the best defense is to beat the enemy's lies with the truth, with prayer, and with the armor of God. That's a big concept to get across in a lesson, so I prepared an outline for a skit and asked the girls to help me. We identified several areas in their lives where the enemy seemed to come in the most, and we wrote a skit based on our results. We dressed up one of the girls in a really cute costume and made the room look like a castle. Another girl dressed in a black sheet and played the enemy. When the enemy came in with a lie, the first girl let her in and then realized that she had fallen for the enemy's lie. In order to defeat him, she studied her Bible and talked to her parents, and did several other things we had identified as enemy busters. Each time she countered with a defense, she became a little bit stronger and got a piece of the armor. We had fun with it and used things like a cowboy hat for the helmet of salvation and a surfboard for the shield of faith. I filmed it and gave each of the girls a DVD. They were thrilled to take it home and show their families.

"I heavily emphasized memorizing Scripture as we went along. One girl was on the dance team at her school, and I commissioned her to write a song using the words to the Scripture passage we were studying and to choreograph a dance routine. I asked her to keep it simple, but it was still hilarious to watch some of us try it! We had a great time and it made memorizing that particular passage much easier!"

| STEP 7: CLOSE WITH ACTION |

In your closing, summarize your lesson and emphasize the moral or main point you want teens to take away. You may want to go around the room and ask them what their main takeaway was from the lesson. Remember, they listen to each other a lot at this age, so one person's positive takeaway may be contagious!

Teens are often eager to live out their faith, so involve them in your prayer time at the end. You may ask one to lead the entire prayer, or you may ask the whole group to participate if they choose to do so. Encourage them to pray for each other, as well.

Showing God's love in the community is a great homework assignment. You might give one of the teens a ten-dollar bill and ask him to put it toward someone's grocery bill as he's standing behind him or her in the grocery line that week. Then have your teen servant come back the next week and report on what he did and the reaction he got. Encourage the teens to "go and do likewise" with their own money, time, or talents.

STEP 7 | EXAMPLE

"We always closed in prayer, but most of my closing activities involved homework," Kassie said. "We each had an assigned prayer partner, and I reminded them to pray for that person each week. And since we had studied about *rhema*, which is a word or truth that God reveals to a person, we formed an Army Girls Rhema Society (ARGR). I assigned one girl for each day of the week to share her *rhema* word with the group through an e-mail. It might be a Scripture or a truth that God revealed in prayer, but it was always encouraging to the rest of us!"

ADULT | STEP 1: CLARIFY OBJECTIVES |

Before you can establish your objectives for your adult class, you must go back to what we discussed at the beginning of the chapter—your role. Are you the primary teacher who teaches every Sunday, or do you rotate with another teacher? Do you occasionally substitute for the teacher in the young adult class, or are you filling in for the next six weeks? You may feel a connection with a certain group of adults and prefer to teach in that area. Perhaps you have a great marriage, and you would like to model your success in a class for young married couples. Have you determined the mission or philosophy for your class, and do you know how it fits with the overall mission of the church?

When you define the objectives for your adult Sunday school class, make sure you seek to understand what God wants to accomplish through you with the group. One of your main objectives, of course, will be to teach the Word of God in the most effective learning environment possible, but God may also lead you to bring cohesiveness or restore harmony to a group that has been through challenges. He may want you to form the college group into a loving, supportive family away from home. Or he may want you to support the mission of the church by teaching Rick Warren's *Forty Days of Purpose.*

What are the actions that you want to happen as a result of this class or series of classes? How do they tie into the bigger message that is being preached and taught throughout your church? Write these objectives down and look at them often to remind yourself why you are teaching and what you want to accomplish.

Once you define your overall objectives, you will need to establish objectives for each week. These, of course, will tie in with your subject matter. Your study of Romans 12:3-8, for example, may be prompted by your objective of exploring spiritual gifts. Or you may have a lot of new Christians in your young adult class, so your study in Romans may focus on walking in love.

STEP 1 | EXAMPLE

My friend Andrew is a pastoral intern at a large church in north Texas, and he directs eighteen married adult classes in the church's Sunday school department. He identified his department's objectives this way: To equip those we are teaching so they can go and disciple others. He explained that they did that through the learning format and through the fellowship or discipleship format. Their goal is to break down the large group of 27,000 people who come to church on Sunday (or Saturday) into smaller units to encourage relationship building, accountability, and discipleship.

| STEP 2: DEFINE YOUR AUDIENCE |

Your class members have their own intrinsic motivation for attending your class, but they are carefully watching how they spend their time and they have certain expectations. Hopefully, they are motivated to attend because of a desire to learn more about the Bible and deepen their walk with the Lord. There may be someone who is motivated to model Sunday school attendance for his family or someone else.

All of these factors affect your members' expectations, so gain as much information about your audience as you can before you start. You may want to poll your students by e-mail, phone, or mail to ask for their expectations. You may even ask some questions about their reasons for attending Sunday school. Listen carefully to discern what issues they are facing at this stage in life.

Consider the demographics of the class members as you build your presentations. Think about the age and stage of life of your group members. Are you teaching young professionals or blue-collar workers? What motivates, frustrates, and inspires them? Also consider the basic spiritual maturity level of your class, their connection with the church, and their level of service. Think about the size of the class you will have and the diversity within it. The more you know about all the distinctions that relate to your audience, the better prepared you can be.

Step 2 | EXAMPLE

The age range for the adults in Andrew's department is forty to fifty-seven. With the variety of ages, there are also life-stage differences. Some of the younger ones still have children at home, while those in the upper part of the age range mostly have grown children.

When new people come into the church, Andrew receives a computer entry giving contact information for those adults that fit into the age group of his classes. He then calls them to introduce himself and welcomes them into the church. During his call, he gathers information about their background, their children, and their interests. He then considers their socio-economic situation, background, and occupation and places them into a class with people with similar life stages and interests. A few of the classes are more of a melting pot, but he finds that most people are more comfortable in a class with people in a similar life stage.

Step 3: Gather Content

Some churches provide a pre-planned curriculum or Bible study for adult classes, but many leave it up to the department head or the teacher to develop or choose the curriculum. Your first resource, of course, is the Bible, but is there a particular version of the Bible that your pastor and leadership recommend? Is there a certain kind of study Bible that would help you with your age group? Many teachers pull their materials from an assortment of different versions, using the excellent study notes that some provide.

If your church does not provide curriculum and you do not feel comfortable developing your own, you can find excellent curriculum at Christian bookstores or online. Standard Publishing (*standardpub.com*) offers a great adult curriculum called *The Standard Lesson Quarterly. Rbpadultministries.org* allows you to download and review a lesson from their curriculum. The *teachsundayschool.com* Web site may have some pretty interesting lessons, as well.

You may be surprised how much material you can glean from your class members. If you find out in your initial questionnaire that someone has a great deal of knowledge about a particular Bible topic, you may be able have this person share his knowledge with the class. Perhaps you have a former missionary in your group. You may want to have her share when you are studying the great commission or the life of Paul. You, as the teacher, are not going to know everything, and the class will probably be excited to hear from someone else from time to time. You are also showing respect for your class members by recognizing their work in God's kingdom and allowing them to contribute.

Step 3 | EXAMPLE

Andrew's department uses curriculum from its denomination's publisher, but the teacher is given liberty as to whether to follow it in the class. "I do think it's great when a teacher uses the published curriculum," he said. "We have a tendency to gravitate toward teaching what we find to be our favorite things, and a curriculum helps to bring a more balanced approach." When Andrew teaches, he uses a variety of content. If he is substituting for a teacher who uses the published curriculum, he continues where the teacher has left off. Since some teachers are lecture-based and some use more engaging techniques, he considers the teacher's style when he is substituting, but he likes to bring as much engagement as he can. Nevertheless, when he teaches a class on his own, Andrew likes to develop his own curriculum. He recently developed a four-week series of discussions for a class he taught.

| Step 4: Maximize Preparation |

Your level of preparation demonstrates the level of respect you have for your students, so start planning your lesson early in the week. If they can tell that you have made an investment in the preparation process, they will be more motivated to participate. Complete the 3-D Outline™ as you plan for your lesson each week. The 3-D Outline™ is just as effective for recurring presentations as it is for one-time speaking engagements. You'll find that the outline will help you focus every week, and it will remind you of the ground you covered in previous lessons.

Write your objectives for the class in the section provided for at the top, and think about the different segments (or *whats*) that will help you achieve those objectives. You may want to start out your class with an attention-grabbing question. Then you can give an overview of the lesson and your objectives for that lesson.

While you are thinking through the segments (the *what*), think about the objectives they relate to (the *why*) and the delivery method (the *how*) you want to use. Will you be using a flip chart to write down major points, or will you prepare a handout that contains information relating to the lesson? Perhaps you want to have someone else in the class present part of the lesson or a short story or testimony, or you may want to include a skit, a role-play, a quiz, or a trivia game. You may want to show part of a video or a movie clip, or you may want to quote a favorite author before a time of discussion.

It's good to keep a file of news reports, magazine articles, or quotes that you find during the week or the quarter that may be relevant to what you are studying. Then you can draw from those resources to use in your class to reinforce your lesson.

If you are teaching a class of young married couples on forgiveness, your 3-D Outline™ may look like this:

3-D OUTLINE™		
Presentation Title:	Forgiving 70 x 7	**Del. Date:**
		06/12
Audience:	Young Married Couples Sunday School Class	**Start Time:**
		9:30 AM
Objectives:	• Grow in understanding of forgiveness from the Scriptures • Gain understanding of consequences of unforgiveness • Gain understanding of the power of forgiveness	**End Time:**
		10:30 AM
Final Preparation Checklist:	[ ] Talk to Jim and Ruth and Ken and Joan about sharing testimonies [ ] Arrange for flip chart	[ ] Prepare and copy handouts

#	Time	What	Why	How	Who
1.	5	Opening: • Purpose • Process • Payoff	Gain buy-in, establish rapport	Talking, handout	Teacher
2.	5	Probing Questions	Set tone for lesson	Talking	Teacher
3.	15	Bible lesson, Part 1: What does the Bible say about forgiveness?	Grow in understanding of forgiveness from scriptural standpoint	Flip chart, Bible, discussion	Teacher
4.	10	Bible lesson, Part 2: What are the consequences of unforgiveness?	Gain understanding of consequences of unforgiveness	Jim and Ruth's testimony/ discussion	Jim and Ruth, class
5.	10	Bible lesson, Part 3: What happens when I forgive?	Gain understanding of the power of forgiveness	Ken and Joan's testimony/ discussion	Ken and Joan, class
6.	15	Closing: Summary, takeaways, call for action	Reinforce lesson	Facilitating	Teacher
	60 min.	**Total Time**			

STEP 4 | EXAMPLE

Andrew encourages his teachers to start preparing early in the week. In fact, he suggests that they begin on Sunday night for the following week! "The first thing that should always happen," he said, "is for them to take a passage, the one set out in the published curriculum or in the curriculum they have designed, and just spend time with the Lord, meditating over that Scripture passage. I encourage them to dive into the text, finding themselves in it. The more they can find themselves in the text, the more apt they are to paint a picture that their audience can also dive into. Then I encourage them to write down any thoughts or ideas they had as they moved through the text. I suggest that they ask themselves questions like, 'What is the situation for the people in the text?' 'What is going on?' 'What is the cultural significance, or is there anything there that stands out as odd?' 'What things in the passage might seem odd or counter-cultural to the people they will be teaching?' As they do that, they generate questions they can look up in the commentaries. I also encourage them to ask the question, 'Where do I see Jesus in the text?' especially if they are studying Old Testament text. Sometimes the Old Testament is really hard for us to bridge for our audiences. So seeing how we see Jesus in the text and making the connection to the New Testament is essential. I encourage them to write down any observations they make about the text and then meditate on that for the next couple of days.

"The most important part of the lesson, for me, is the application. And application has to have a bridge of illustration for it to really be powerful. So I suggest that the teachers start looking early in the week for things in our culture, in society, on television, or on the radio that they can use to apply the truth of the text they are teaching. When they identify those things, pull them out, and save them, they become the jewels of the lesson, because they are the very things that will bring this ancient text into the now. Bringing the Word of God into the now is the most important function a preacher or teacher has in the church.

"I suggest to our teachers that in the middle or the latter part of the week, they go through and read the commentaries on the text they will be teaching and develop an outline. The outline will include the application that will bring the text from the then into the now for their students."

| STEP 5: OPEN WELL |

Meeting and greeting people as they come through the door is always a great way to start for any age level. With adults, it's good to be direct and upfront about your objectives and agenda. You may want to have your lesson plan or agenda written on a flip chart and review it at the beginning of the class. Or you may want to have a handout with the major points you will be covering.

STEP 5 | EXAMPLE

"In the opening, it is important to be specific and relevant, both to the text and to the people in my audience," Andrew said. "I look for an illustration that is both emotion-grabbing and that ties in well. One of my favorite ways to open is to find a story in the media that has occurred that week, so it is fresh on my audience members' minds.

"I also like to find illustrations that are powerful pictures, so I might Google images on a specific topic. Recently I found a picture of an Indonesian boy caught paddling in the ocean with one arm! My topic was the hope we can have in Christ, even in the midst of hard circumstances. I blew up the picture and held it in front of my class and asked, 'What do you see?' Then I gave them a minute. (It's important for a teacher to be okay with an awkward silence.) The picture was powerful enough to evoke thoughts and emotions, so the audience members just started throwing out words and descriptions. Then I tied it into my Bible text by saying something like, 'You know, we all find ourselves in these situations. Sometimes we are caught in a boat in the middle of an ocean, where we are paddling with only one arm. In the gospel of Matthew, chapter 8, we find another person who feels the same way.' Then I gave my background on the text, along with my thesis statement."

| STEP 6: ENGAGE YOUR AUDIENCE |

In order to keep your class members from "zoning out," you have to keep their minds from wandering and keep them connected to what you are saying. In today's world, people are bombarded with information, so you will need to think of ways to help them focus and connect with the lesson you are presenting. You cannot compete with the multimillion-dollar budgets that back today's media, and you do not really need to. Involve your audience with thoughtful questions, new information, and creative engagement to keep them connected to you and your presentation.

Some of the most effective presenters alive today present well by letting their passion flow. We have probably all known Sunday school teachers, for example, who do not use a variety of activities and presentation methods, but they keep people on the edge of their seats because of their passion for the messages they are presenting. When you are speaking out of that kind of passion, you usually weave in stories and personal testimonies that have contributed to your passion. I honestly don't know if anyone can go overboard on having passion for his subject. In fact, we all want to ask God to inspire us and help us to speak out of that passion. I say, let it flow. But it is great, too, to allow the adults in your class to have a shared-learning experience by providing some time for sharing, discussion and, feedback.

STEP 6 | EXAMPLE

Andrew shared, "I format my talk where I have the opening illustration, then an explanation of the text, another illustration, and an application section. There are two areas where I engage my audience the most: in the explanation of the text and in the application section. In the explanation of the text, I like to loosen them up by asking simple background questions about the Bible, things I am sure they will know. Then I give them positive affirmations for answering correctly, and it builds their confidence. By the time we get to the application question at the end, they are more apt to participate because we have connected emotionally through the positive affirmations and the illustration. I spend a lot of time crafting my application questions. I try to make sure they are specific, yet open-ended enough for my students to really dive into.

"For my illustration, I look for something that pertains to the truth we are discussing and something that connects with the audience, either in a current-event way or emotionally. Sometimes I use poems or song lyrics. By using a song that I know many of them listen to, I connect with them. By the time I apply the text to the song and their lives, I have brought it into the now in a powerful way. As they are thinking about that truth,

I ask the application question. Then I pause and look directly at them. I usually find that one audience member speaks, and then another, until the sharing begins to snowball. I allow them to continue sharing and just direct them to move through the points we have discussed."

| STEP 7: CLOSE WITH ACTION |

My favorite way to close a teaching is to go around the room and ask people to give their main takeaway from the lesson or tell what they are going to do differently as a result of this lesson. If your class is larger, you may just pick people out of the group and ask them or ask for people to raise their hands to answer that question. With the various answers given, your main points will probably be reviewed and your lesson reinforced.

STEP 7 | EXAMPLE

"The closing is really important," Andrew shared. "I try to be inspirational. Even if it was a hard lesson, I want my audience members to leave knowing that they are the hands and feet of Jesus, and that what God has done in their lives that day has equipped them to change the world. I usually give them a charge. I commission them to go and be different—whether it is different in abstaining from something or different in engaging in something—and I encourage them to start moving in that direction. I like to sandwich my introduction and my conclusion. When I used the picture of the Indonesian boy, for example, I held the picture up again during the closing and said something like, 'We are in the boat. Sometimes we feel like we are paddling with one arm, because of the hard times we are going through (and I named some things they may be going through). But we don't have to feel like we are paddling alone anymore.' Then I charged them to take the things they learned and go out and live it."

I want to thank you—whether you are a Sunday school teacher, Bible study teacher, youth or children's ministry teacher, vacation Bible school teacher, or workshop teacher—for what you are doing to make such an incredible impact on the lives of the people you teach. Your ripple of influence will spread far and wide, and I pray that your reward in Heaven will be great.

SCENARIO 4 VIP'S

! As a teacher you have the awesome opportunity, with the Holy Spirit working through you, to transform lives.

! It is important for Sunday school teachers to grow in their own walks with the Lord, pray for wisdom, and pursue knowledge and skills that will help them be as effective as possible.

! Begin working on your lesson early in the week. Waiting until Saturday night to prepare puts undue pressure on you, stifles your creativity, and does not allow you adequate time to think and pray about what God wants to say through you.

YOUNG CHILDREN:

! When teaching young children, your objectives may include:

- Building a strong, supportive relationship with each child and his or her parents
- Praying for your students and their salvation
- Actively involving parents in their child's spiritual development
- Cascading the Sunday school message to the children's families and friends
- Helping the children grow in their understanding and knowledge of God and who Jesus is

! The age range of the children you will be teaching is the most important consideration in defining your audience. Also consider their background, frame of reference, and attention span.

! Start the lesson with a teaser to get the children excited about what they will be doing.

! Toys and props make great tools for helping younger children connect with the Bible story.

TEENS:

! When teaching teens, your objectives may include:

- Finding ways to make your class time so enjoyable and meaningful for them that they will want to come back week after week with their friends
- Building a strong, supportive relationship with each student
- Helping your teens grow in their knowledge and understanding of the Lord

! As you teach teens, it is important to consider their age, maturity level, background, and interests.

! As you choose or develop your own curriculum, you will want to filter in the teens' expectations and interests, but not at the expense of biblical integrity or alignment with the mission of your church and denomination.

! Teens often interpret lack of preparation as lack of caring.

! Look for creative ways to get teens to participate in the delivery as well as the learning. You may even want to have some of the teens present the Bible lesson or report back on an assignment you gave the week before.

ADULTS:

! When you define the objectives for your adult Sunday school class, make sure you seek to understand what God wants to accomplish through you with the group.

! Your class members have their own intrinsic motivation for attending your class, but they are carefully watching how they spend their time, and they have certain expectations.

! Gain as much information about your audience as you can before you start. You may want to poll your students to find out their expectations, their reasons for attending Sunday school, and what issues they are facing at this stage in life.

! Involve your audience with thoughtful questions, new information, and creative engagement to keep them connected to you and your presentation.

! Some of the most effective presenters alive today present well by letting their passion flow. We all want to ask God to inspire us and help us to speak out of that passion.

6. Denise Oliveri, "What Makes a Good Sunday School Teacher," ideamarketers.com, http://www.ideamarketers.com/?What_Makes_a_Good_Sunday_School_Teacher&articleid=351065 (accessed October 7, 2008). Used by permission.

7. Kathleen Fuller, "How to Teach a Teen Sunday School Class," ehow.com, "http://www.ehow.com/how_2177399_teach-teen-sunday-school-class.html (accessed October 10, 2008).

8. Kelli Mahoney, "Tips for Running a Good Bible Study for Teens," about.com, http://christianteens.about.com/od/biblestudyresources/a/runningbibstudy.htm (accessed October 10, 2008)

9. Kimberly L. Keith, "Ideas for Vacation Bible School," about.com, http://childparenting.about.com/cs/k6education/a/vacationbible.htm (accessed October 8, 2008).

TRAIN OTHERS

> Instruct a wise man and he will be wiser still; teach a righteous man and he will add to his learning.

—PROVERBS 9:9

The Greek word *ekklesia* was used in ancient Rome to name a public gathering. In the New Testament, the word pointed to an assembly and is translated as "church" in most Bible translations. Broken down into its root, the word means to be called out. The church is the only institution founded by Jesus. He has called us out of the trappings of this world to advance God's will on earth through the gathering of the church. Through all its difficulties, shortcomings, and failures, God still loves, empowers, and uses the *ekklesia*.

The power and hope of the church rests on this gathering of volunteers doing what we can to faithfully serve our Lord. The assembly of the church can only reach as far as its members are willing to extend their gifts, talents, and hands. The vast majority of us in the church are not professional staff members. And the vast majority of the work of the church happens through men and women who are eager and called, but not necessarily trained.

Have you ever been in a church or ministry setting where everything seemed to run smoothly? Maybe you were at a large ministry conference where things seemed to flow perfectly, the crowds were organized, and the follow-up was flawless. Perhaps you have been at a church where the greeters were gracious and welcoming, the teachers were effective and caring, the facilities were clean and well kept, and the nursery workers were loving and nurturing. Show me a ministry like that—whether it is a church or another organization—and I will show you a ministry that understands the enormous value of training its volunteers.

Every volunteer within an organization has an opportunity to present the pulse of the ministry—and the one it represents—to those who enter its doors. A well-oiled organization trains its members in procedures, practices, and protocols so that everyone in every position in the ministry is operating from the same page and speaking the same vision through his or her words and actions. Through effective training, the church ensures that its DNA is clearly seen throughout the entire organization. You may be in a church or ministry organization that recognizes the impact volunteer training has on its effectiveness. Perhaps you have even conducted such training yourself a number of times. Or maybe volunteer training is something new to you. Regardless of your church's experience with training, this chapter will give you the opportunity to raise the bar for your organization.

In this chapter, we will look at specific principles for more effective training. We will talk about how people learn and look at some questioning techniques and listening skills. As we go through the *Seven Steps to Effective Presentations* and see how they apply to the training process, we will also address the weightier issue of *speaking the same vision*.

| How People Learn |

Several years ago I coauthored a workshop on training adult learners, called *Training Other People to Train*. In that workshop manual, we suggested that several principles apply when working with adult learners. These principles were first developed for a corporate setting, but they certainly apply to volunteers in ministry as well. Adult learners:

! Like to be part of the learning experience through discussion or through group interaction
! Learn effectively from peers
! Learn more efficiently when their unique learning style is predominant
! Monitor their own learning and discover their own answers
! Learn pragmatically through hands-on exercises and involvement
! Favor different sensory modes for learning

Do any of these learning principles ring true for you? Let's take a closer look at the last item on the list. There are three primary sensory modes of learning: visual, auditory, and kinesthetic (or hands-on). When we talk about sensory modes for learning, we just mean that different people learn in different ways. You can employ all three modes for learning in almost every presentation you give.

The participant who is primarily visual learns better by seeing something. Your explanation of a process will confuse and frustrate the visual leaner unless you provide extra visual tools such as:

! charts
! graphs
! diagrams
! videos
! slides
! handouts

The primarily auditory participant learns better by listening. Visual aids can be helpful, but they are not essential. If you want to reach an auditory learner, incorporate presentation tools and techniques like:

! verbal presentation
! storytelling
! discussion
! question-and-answer sessions
! videos
! reporting

A participant who is primarily kinesthetic learns better by taking part in a hands-on process. Kinesthetic learners are often adept at athletics, dance, and other activities that require muscle memory. You can reach kinesthetic learners through things like:

! group exercises
! simulations
! role-playing
! group projects
! practice

Most people respond to a mixture of these three modes of learning, but everyone has a favorite. By designing your training to include a variety of these sensory modes, you can create a more positive learning experience for virtually all of your volunteers. For example, a training session that includes a presentation for the auditory learner, incorporates a detailed handout for the visual learner, and closes with role-playing for the kinesthetic learner would optimize learning for almost all of your participants.

Regardless of learning styles, the adults you are training go through four basic stages of learning. As you train the volunteers within your ministry organization, remember that your audience is moving through the four following stages at varying rates.

1. **Unconscious Incompetence** At this stage, learners do not know the concept, principle, or fact that you are relating. And they also do not realize that they don't know. Consider the time before you knew how to drive a car. As you watched your parents drive, you may have thought, "I can do that." But when you first sat behind the wheel, you began to realize your ignorance.

2. **Conscious Incompetence** In this stage, learners know that they are incompetent. Perhaps when you first got behind the wheel, you hit the accelerator too hard and ran over the garbage can. Suddenly you realized how much you had to learn about driving. Recognizing what you need to know is a positive step toward learning it.

3. **Conscious Competence** At this stage, learners can perform a skill, practice, or process only by paying a great deal of attention to it. As a beginning driver, you had to pay special attention to maneuvers like shifting, turning, using signals, and braking.

4. **Unconscious Competence** At this stage, people can perform a task easily and without thinking about it. When you drive up to a stop sign at this point in your life, hopefully you do not say to yourself, "Now where is the brake?" The task is performed smoothly and without conscious effort. This mastery is the final goal of training. Unconscious competence allows you to complete the task without having to pay a great deal of attention to the job. It has become something like a habit.

You will be training your people in the procedures, practices, and protocols established by your ministry organization. The more *unconscious competence* they have in those applications, the more attention they can give to their spiritual service to people. There are many skills that you may be teaching them, such as people skills and listening skills, which should become second nature to them through unconscious competence. I want to be careful to say here that your goal with your ministry volunteers is not to have them mindlessly going through the motions of getting the job done. If your volunteers are not putting their hearts and souls into their jobs, something is wrong.

| QUESTIONING AND LISTENING TECHNIQUES |

As a trainer, you may feel pressure to provide all of the content for your audience. Let me suggest that you facilitate your participants' learning process by incorporating two very important tools as you train: questioning and listening.

Meaningful questions provide powerful learning opportunities. When you are training, asking questions can sometimes be more effective than just presenting. You can use well-crafted questions to accomplish the following purposes:

1. To gather information. "How have we done that in the past?"
2. To lead or guide the conversation. "You did it that way for a reason, didn't you?"
3. To subtly put the conversational responsibility back on the other person. "What would you do?"
4. To encourage thought. "What do you think about that?"
5. To focus the conversation. "Why is that so?"
6. To encourage new ideas and thoughts. "What do you all think about that concept?" "Who wants to go first?"
7. To close a discussion. "Is there anything else anyone wants to add?"
8. To ensure that everyone understands what is being said or communicated. "What is the main thing you got out of our session today?"

As you craft your questions to achieve the purposes described above, there are several different types of questions you can use. As you choose the type of questions to use, think about how long you want the discussion to go, the depth of processing needed, the size of your audience, and the transition you plan to make to the next section. Incorporate a variety of the following question types:

! Closed question—one that requires a specific answer, such as a yes or no or a correct response to a test question. For example, "Are you comfortable greeting people you don't know?"

❗ Open-ended question—one that calls for a thoughtful response or requests information. For example, "How would you go about greeting someone you don't know?"

❗ General overview question—one that is proposed to the entire group rather than being directed to a particular person. It's often used to initiate a discussion or to set up a thoughtful exercise. For example, "How important is it for a visitor to be warmly greeted and made to feel welcome?"

❗ Direct question—one that is asked of a particular individual, which allows you to capture someone's attention, involve someone who has not participated, or redirect the flow of conversation if necessary. For example, "How would you direct that person, Tim?"

❗ Return question—one that puts the question back to the questioner or to the group, perhaps to establish a particular volunteer's expertise. For example, "What do you think about that procedure, Hannah?" "Does anyone have a response to that question?"

Listening is just as much a part of communication as speaking. In fact, understanding between the two parties will not take place until both the presenter and audience member have heard one another. When you are training your ministry volunteers, remember that your participants will be sending spoken and unspoken messages throughout your entire training experience. You will be a much more effective presenter and trainer when you capture the art of listening.

As a volunteer is talking, ask yourself, "Am I really listening or am I simply waiting for my turn to talk?" If you are thinking about your reply before the other person is finished, then you are not listening at the top level. You will become a more effective listener if you apply the following strategies as you listen to your audience members:

1. Be attentive. As simple as this sounds, we sometimes have to remind ourselves to pay attention to what a person is saying.
2. Quietly observe. Remain silent and maintain eye contact with the speaker. Stay focused.
3. Acknowledge. Periodically respond to the speaker with phrases like "I see" or "I'm following you."
4. Summarize and give feedback. Restate what you think the other person is saying. "So what I understand you are saying is . . ."

Now let us link the effective training, questioning, and listening skills together while we apply the *Seven Steps to Effective Presentations* to the training scenario.

| STEP 1: CLARIFY OBJECTIVES |

When you are defining your objectives for your training session, decide what you want your training to accomplish. In any training scenario, there are generally four different outcomes—or a combination thereof—that you want to accomplish: raising awareness, training a skill, transferring knowledge, or changing a behavior or attitude.

Let's consider the scenario of training greeters for your ministry or church. If you are teaching your greeters that they represent the spirit and personality of your church when they greet with a great smile, you are addressing awareness. If you are training them to quickly relate to people as they come in and make them feel welcome, then you are training them in a skill. If you are teaching them the procedure for directing people to the various classes or ministry departments, then you are transferring knowledge. If you have an update in vision, the ministry's protocols may have changed and you may have to deal with changing a behavior or attitude. Whether you are training for one of these outcomes or a combination of them in your training session, your objectives will be determined by the outcomes you wish to achieve.

When you are training volunteers of any ministry organization, it is *very important* that your training objectives align with the objectives of your organization. Every detail of your training should flow with the vision of the ministry. Imagine that you were training volunteers who will greet at a large ministry conference. How would you train them to respond if a person asked a question about the beliefs of your organization? Every volunteer greeter should be given a copy of the organization's beliefs and be well versed in how to respond to those questions. How would your organization's vision statement dictate that you respond to a person who comes to your volunteers with an emotional need? Should the volunteer direct the person to an outside agency or to a staff person? If the greeters are handling a situation one way and the ushers or parking-lot attendants are handling it a different way, they are not *speaking from the same vision!* Hopefully, the leadership's vision has cascaded throughout the organization, and you are reinforcing that vision with all of your training objectives.

Cascading is another matter that you need to consider. How will your training be cascaded throughout the organization? Will you train the "end user," or will you train people who train others? For example, the associate pastor of a church may train three people who are over all of the small groups. Those three may, in turn, train all of the small group leaders. If you are training trainers, your objectives need to include a process that makes it easy for them to cascade the training to someone else. This will maximize effectiveness and consistency in your group. Detailed handouts are great tools for cascading.

STEP 1 | EXAMPLE

Bill Arnold, a good friend and spiritual mentor, asked me to conduct a training session on presentation skills for about one hundred staff members and volunteers at the church he attends. I used the training seminar I developed from my book *Inspire Any Audience.* I had two primary objectives:

1. Deliver value for my friend, who has done so much for me.
2. Deliver value for each of the attendees in the form of effective presentation skills he or she could apply in their own ministry circumstances.

| STEP 2: DEFINE YOUR AUDIENCE |

As you develop your training, consider the age, maturity level, and the level of understanding your audience has regarding your subject. Are they seasoned volunteers or just starting out? Have they ever volunteered in this area before? As you prepare your training, it is especially important to consider your audience's experience level. While you may consider some concepts as common knowledge or even tired ideas, the information may be enlightening and fresh to the novice in ministry. If your volunteers are more experienced, too much focus on foundational concepts may frustrate and bore them.

STEP 2: | EXAMPLE

I asked Bill to help me define my audience. He gave me information about the audience members that helped me understand the level of their experience and their current presentation skills. I also polled my audience members after I arrived, which gave me better clarity about them and their expectations.

| STEP 3: GATHER CONTENT |

Your first source for training material should be the leadership of your ministry. Visit with the person on your leadership team who is over your department to pick his brain. Ask questions and take notes about vision, objectives, procedures, and protocols. Then design your training material accordingly. If there is no one on your leadership team or on staff who can help you develop your content, find someone who may be your counterpart at another similar ministry to help you.

As you develop your content, remember the three different kinds of learners—the visual, auditory, and kinesthetic—so you can include segments that allow you to reach all three styles.

If you are training volunteers who will be cascading the information to others, provide very comprehensive handouts that contain all the information they will need to share. In a training setting, handouts accomplish several things: They establish consistency for the group, they optimize learning as the participants follow along during class, and they perpetuate the training when participants refer back to them for review.

STEP 3 | EXAMPLE

Bill had shared with his team my expertise in helping people improve their presentation skills. They had read my *Inspire Any Audience* book and were aware of the seminar content. When I developed the seminar, I designed it with the different learning styles in mind and included activities that appealed to all three.

I had conducted the seminar many times before with proven results. I customized about five percent of the seminar to fit the particular needs of that audience. Several years ago, I had co-developed a video series on the *Inspire Any Audience* content with my friend and colleague, Zig Ziglar. Since it is well known that Zig is strong in his Christian faith, I knew my audience would relate to him. I included video clips highlighting Zig's presentations to reinforce and strengthen my message.

| STEP 4: MAXIMIZE PREPARATION |

In Chapter 1 I talked about the concept of planned spontaneity. As the trainer, you are considered an expert on the subject matter you are teaching. If you are not, become one! Fill up your "information cushion" by reading as much as you can find on the subject and by talking to others whom you consider expert. You will not use it all in your presentation, but in a training setting you will probably have questions that go beyond the material you present. Anticipate as many questions as you can, and then find the answers. It is okay to say you don't know the answers to one or two questions, but if that is your response for very many, you will lose credibility.

Engage the strategic thinking process by examining your objectives to come up with the *what* and *how* properties of your presentation. Develop your 3-D Outline™ and then make your checklist to remind you of all the tactical tasks that need to be done. Develop and copy the handouts for your participants well in advance so you will not be pressured by time. If someone else will be sharing during your presentation, ask him well in advance so he will have time to prepare, as well. Make sure he knows the parameters of his part in the presentation so he will not over or under prepare. Gather any videos, props, or visual aids you will be using. Arrange for audio-visual equipment. Prepare any flip charts you can in advance. Plan for food or beverages for breaks, and remember the music if that is part of your strategy.

Decide early on how you want your training room set up, and then communicate those arrangements to the person who will be doing it. If that happens to be you, set up the room the day before if possible. Become comfortable with the room. See where you will be standing and sit where your audience members will be sitting to gain their perspective. Check all equipment the day before, and then go early to check it again on the day of your training.

Let's see what your 3-D Outline™ may look like for a presentation on training greeters for a ministry convention.

3-D OUTLINE™				
Presentation Title:	Greeter Training		**Del. Date:**	
			05 /10	
Audience:	Volunteer Greeters		**Start Time:**	
			9:30 AM	
Objectives:	• Set tone for ministry • Communicate vision • Provide tactical instruction • Elevate participants' people skills • Help participants feel comfortable in role		**End Time:** 10:30 AM	
Final Preparation Checklist:	[ ] Copy handouts [ ] Test equipment [ ] Arrange for flip chart and markers			
#	**Time**	**What**	**Why**	**How**	**Who**
1.	5	Opening: • Welcome • Purpose (Objectives) • Process (Agenda) • Payoff (Benefits)	Establish rapport, gain buy-in	Presenting	Presenter
2.	15	Discuss ministry opportunities/ people skills	Set ministry tone, elevate people skills	Facilitating/ flip chart	Presenter and participants
3.	20	Review procedures, practices, and protocols	Provide tactical instruction, communicate vision	Handout	Presenter
4.	15	Role-play (3 scenarios)	Facilitate comfort, elevate people skills	Role-play	6 participants
5.	5	Closing: ask for takeaways	Solidify learning	Facilitating	Presenter and participants
	60 min. **Total Time**				

Step 4 | EXAMPLE

I called Bill to make arrangements for the audio-visual equipment and room setup. I asked him to describe the room to me, and I envisioned where I would be standing. Then I arrived early to get comfortable with the room, make adjustments as needed, and test out the equipment. Since I had presented this seminar many times before, I knew the material well and was comfortable with my information cushion. I took copies of participant materials and the props I use during the seminar.

Here is a copy of the 3-D Outline™ I developed for the *Inspire Any Audience* seminar:

3-D OUTLINE™				
Presentation Title:	Inspire Any Audience		**Date:**	
Audience:			**Location:**	
Objectives:	• Teach how to use creative energy and technical knowledge to create impact and influence others • Elevate attendee's persuasive skills	• Train to inspire loyalty and commitment when presenting		
#	**Time**	**What**	**Why**	**How**
	15	**Final Prep** ❑ Confirm equipment on site (i.e. LCD projector) ❑ Pack and bring materials for 10 attendees	To assure that everything is in place and working	List, set up, and test

#	Time	What	Why	How
1.	45	**Intro/Bio** **Introduction** • Purpose (Objectives) • Process (Agenda) • Payoff (Benefits) • **Most Common Presentations** • Expectations **(What you would most like to get out of this course)**	Let the participants know who we are, why we are here, and why they should listen to us. Grab attention, build rapport, and gain focus for our time together	Present/Fun factor Slides Notetaker (and review "The Psychology of Persuasion and Influence")
	60	**Presentation Quiz**	Set up direction to maximize everyone's time for this course	
	15	**Floating Break as needed**		
2.	15	**Bombed & Best**	Gain audience involvement and get participants thinking about what makes a good presentation	Facilitate Pair Activity and Report Out
3.	15	**CPA Presentation Model and Elements**	Show the value of not just delivery skills improvement, but knowing the audience, the content, the before and after elements	F/C Discussion
4.	45	• The 4 Levels of Learning **7 Foundational Secrets (from IAA Book)** 1. The Funneling Process 2. Opening (incl. audience types & setting the tone) 3. Alleviate the 4 Audience Tensions 4. Trust Transference	Teach the 7 basic items to include in any presentation. Define 4 audience types & objectives. Show Zig video to give clear example, establish some trust transference, and add variety to the presentation	Show video clip of Zig Ziglar opening
	15	**Floating Break as needed**		
5.	15	**7 Foundational Secrets (continued)** 5. Business Entertainment™ 6. Verbal Surveying 7. Targeted Polling • Audience Closure		Show video clip of Zig audience involved

#	Time	What	Why	How
6.	20	**Live Example of a 3-D Outline™**	Demonstrate in real-time how helpful and easy a 3-D Outline™ is to create	Facilitate the creation of the 3-D Outline™ with one of the audience members.
LUNCH (Begin here or after segment 7)				
7.	60	Build Your Own 3-D Outline™ • Pairs develop outline for real life presentation • (Incorporating 5+ ideas from morning session) • Share Examples	Allow participants the opportunity to immediately apply 3-D Outline™ tool and other workshop ideas and concepts to real life. Share examples and ideas with the group	Facilitator supported individual work (perhaps in pairs if appropriate) Individual report outs
8.	60	**Report Out 3-D Outlines™**	Further learn the process and pick up ideas from others in the course	Report outs
9.	60-120	**Present to Group with Peer Critique**	Put to use the ideas and concepts shared so far and further gain ideas to be your best while presenting	Tony facilitates - ❑ Prepare approx. 10 min presentations using the 3-D Outline™ ❑ Attendees deliver the presentation with peer critique on 3 x 5 cards Discuss each presentation as a whole group with Tony's suggestions
10.	15	**Optional Open Forum**	Catch any expectations that were not covered	Facilitated Discussion
11.	30	**Closing / Summarize**	Review	Tony facilitates
12.	15	**Action activity / Evaluate and Close**	Clarify actions to take	Action cards In-house evaluations.
	8 hrs.	**Total Time**		

| STEP 5: OPEN WELL |

In a training scenario, questions that help you assess your audience's current level of mastery of your subject provide great openers. You can simply ask questions like, "How many of you know this?" or "How many of you have thought about this?" Opening with questions gets both you and your volunteers warmed up, and it sets the tone for the meeting as you communicate through questions. You can also open with a true story about how the area of training or ministry has changed a life or made an impact on the overall ministry or organization. Starting with the end result will help your audience see how valuable your training is.

STEP 5 | EXAMPLE

I asked Bill to introduce me. He is a professional presenter and a member of that church, so I leveraged that connection. Then I set the tone for involvement right away by asking questions like, "How do you feel about presentations?" "How many presentations do you make each month?" "What kind of presentations do you make?" As people raised their hands, I called on them to respond.

| STEP 6: ENGAGE YOUR AUDIENCE |

You want to continue involving your audience throughout your presentation. Call the participants by name and maintain eye contact with one person at a time. Remember to talk to individuals instead of to the masses. Ask your participants to write something down. Use humor if you are so inclined, or at least encourage it in the extroverts in your audience. Remember to reward participation with sincere compliments.

Your participants will be involved during much of your training session with the handouts you have prepared. Open-ended questions are also very effective in a training setting. They stimulate thinking and encourage involvement. You might ask, "How do you think people would respond to that?" or "Why do you think this might work?" Incorporate various *Strategic Engagement* activities like quizzes, video clips, PowerPoint presentations, stories, or anecdotes. Role-playing is an especially productive tool for training.

STEP 6 | EXAMPLE

I had set the tone for involvement in my opening, and I continued that interaction throughout the training. I encouraged questions and facilitated humor from those participants who exhibited that tendency. I also gave away dollar bills to reward participation, the *Strategic Engagement* activity that has been an audience favorite over the years. Several times during the training, I broke the audience into pairs or small groups for different activities, such as preparing their first 3-D Outline™.

| STEP 7: CLOSE WITH ACTION |

You want to make sure that your action-oriented objectives have been met. Your audience is full of volunteers, of course. You cannot demand that they take action, but you can compel and encourage them toward it. You can also get feedback from the audience members to make sure they understand what you have taught. In fact, you should make sure that understanding has taken place before you end the session. You can do that by asking questions, asking for takeaways, or providing a time for a question and answer session with the audience.

STEP 7 | EXAMPLE

I summarized my main points and asked for takeaways. Then I handed out action cards and asked the participants to write on them the things they wanted to take action on as a result of what they learned during the training seminar. I suggested that they keep the cards in their wallets to remind them of their commitment to action.

As a trainer for a ministry in the church, you have a great opportunity to help Christians fulfill their call to serve. It is a very important function, and the need is great. Thank you for your part in equipping the saints for works of service!

SCENARIO 5 VIP'S

! The vast majority of us in the church are not professional staff members. And the vast majority of the work of the church happens through men and women who are eager and called, but not necessarily trained.

! Through effective training, the church ensures that its DNA is clearly seen throughout the entire organization.

! Adults go through four stages of learning at varying rates: unconscious incompetence, conscious incompetence, conscious competence, and unconscious competence.

! When you are training, asking questions can sometimes be more effective than just presenting.

! You will be a much more effective presenter and trainer when you capture the art of listening.

! In any training scenario, there are generally four different outcomes—or a combination thereof—that you want to accomplish: raising awareness, training a skill, transferring knowledge, or changing a behavior or attitude.

! As you develop your training, consider the age, maturity level, level of understanding about your subject, and the experience level of your audience members.

! There are three primary sensory modes of learning: visual, auditory, and kinesthetic (or hands-on). As you develop your content, include segments that allow you to reach all three styles.

LEAD A GREAT MEETING

> Then make my joy complete by being like-minded, having the same love, being one in spirit and purpose. Do nothing out of selfish ambition or vain conceit, but in humility consider others better than yourselves. Each of you should look not only to your own interests, but also to the interests of others.

—PHILIPPIANS 2:2-4

If you have been involved in activities within your church for any length of time, you know that meetings are a fact of life. I have even heard them called a "necessary evil." Perhaps that is because meetings, in both the corporate and ministry worlds, are not always as productive as they should be.

You have likely witnessed that many of the great accomplishments that happen in ministry are birthed and shaped in meetings. Many critical and far-reaching issues are addressed in meetings, like vision and organizational direction, budget and staffing decisions, policy decisions, and strategic planning. Other meetings offer opportunities to identify the need for change, promote vision continuity, and rally people around a cause. Since so much is at stake, it is important to diligently prepare for and conduct good, productive meetings.

In the world of ministry we often have both limited time and limited resources. We have to work around the schedules of all of the other volunteers involved—not to mention our own hectic schedules. I want to encourage you to apply the processes we are sharing in this chapter to effectively use the time you have. Not every meeting has to be perfect. In fact, one of my mottos is to strive for excellence, not perfection—and there is a big difference. The atmosphere we set for a meeting greatly impacts the outcome, the morale of those attending, and even the participants' desire to continue volunteering their time and effort.

If a meeting is handled well, there is a certain synergy created that produces amazing results. The word *synergy* comes from the Greek word *synergo* (meaning "working together") and is a term used to describe a situation where the final outcome of a system is greater than the sum of its parts. [10] The apostle Paul used the Greek word twice in his epistles. In Romans 8:28, Paul writes, "And we know that God causes everything to work together for the good of those who love God and are called according to his purpose for them" (NLT). God causes everything to work together to bring about positive results in our lives. In 1 Corinthians 3:6, Paul said that he planted the seed, Apollos watered it, and God made it grow. In verse 9, he said, "For we are God's fellow workers." When people work together in meetings, the synergy that is produced can bring about positive results that could not be achieved by someone working alone.

In a little book called *Meeting Magic* that I coauthored with George Lowe a few years ago, we put it another way: "Have you ever seen a famous magician perform? Seemed like you were watching a one-person show, didn't it? But you weren't. In reality, you were watching a TEAM perform: stage assistants, lighting and special effects people, sound technicians…as well as the magician. Sure, the magician may wave the wand and pull the rabbit out of the hat, but the real secret to making magic is a bunch of people all working together. A meeting is a lot like a magic show. You have a group of people trying to reach a common goal. If you have good leadership and share the work, you can produce results that appear magical."

People often think that when they attend a meeting, it is up to the leader to make things happen. I would like to propose a change in thinking. If you're in a meeting as a participant or a leader, you can look for ways to contribute so that the meeting will be a win for everyone. It's important to be a good meeting leader, but it's equally important to be a good meeting participant. Rather than feeling sorry for the leader who is struggling, look for ways to help. For example, you may want to make a comment or two to give him a moment of breathing space. Isn't that really what being part of the same family, the family of God, is all about? When you step in to make the meeting a winning situation for everyone, you are obeying God's direction in Ephesians 4:32, to "be kind and compassionate to one another."

Whether you are attending a meeting or leading it, your attitude and actions can make a big difference. There are two main reasons why leaders do not conduct good meetings. The first is they do not have good processes. The second is that they procrastinate in their preparation. In this chapter, I want to help you work through these stumbling blocks. As we go through the *Seven Steps to Effective Presentations,* I will teach you the good meeting processes that my team and I have developed and taught to thousands in the corporate world.

| STEP 1: CLARIFY OBJECTIVES |

Too often an agenda is established for a meeting without clear objectives in mind. We have all probably been to meetings where there seemed to be no objective at all. There may have been a great deal of discussion that took place, but nothing was decided and no action was taken or even defined.

To lead an effective meeting, you must decide where you want to go and how you want to get there. The objectives will drive your meeting. You can develop your objectives by considering the desired outcomes of your meeting. For example, your desired outcome may be for your Sunday school teachers to understand the curriculum for the next quarter. Your objective would be to review and discuss the curriculum. Or your desired outcome may be to have an effective outreach to the homeless in your community. Your objective for the meeting would be to design a working program and come up with a plan to implement it.

You may want to build some of your objectives around your defined audience. For example, if you are having a budget and finance meeting and you know that some of your volunteer participants are not well versed in that area, one of your objectives may be to give the participants a frame of reference for the ministry's accounting methodology. If you are having a large meeting to deal with a zoning issue for a new property, you may think about which members of your audience know about zoning. If someone came to mind, one of your objectives may be to hear from selected participants who can share expertise about zoning requirements.

STEP 1 | EXAMPLE

The church my family and I attended had most of the elements in place for tremendous growth. We needed a plan to position the church in the community from a branding perspective. I hosted a brainstorming meeting of key leaders in the church, some staff and some volunteers, to develop a plan and devise a strategy for implementation. These were our objectives:

1. To share some of the branding strategies I use in business and merge them with ideas from others in the group.
2. Better define where we were going as a church and develop a strategy for positioning its brand in the community.

| STEP 2: DEFINE YOUR AUDIENCE |

In a ministry situation you may be given the opportunity to choose your team and the participants in your meetings, or the participants may be selected for you by tradition or history, appointment, or a vote. Whatever the case, think through what your participants have in common. Hopefully they are all marching to the same vision. They likely all have some interest or stake in the ministry or meeting topic. Do they have knowledge or experience that will contribute to the desired outcomes? Perhaps some of your participants are just eager to serve. If so, they will probably end up with several action items by the end of the meeting!

STEP 2 | EXAMPLE

Based on the objectives, we knew we needed to involve the church's leadership team as well as several businesspeople from the church who had experienced success in branding their own businesses. We invited six or seven people to participate in the brainstorming meeting. The split between staff and volunteers was about even.

| STEP 3: GATHER CONTENT |

The content for your meeting may come from a variety of sources. Your content, of course, will revolve around your agenda. Sometimes that content may come from past meeting notes, a specific team member who has conducted research, or from relevant documents or facts surrounding the topic. As the leader, you may need to do some research yourself in order to present an item on the agenda; or you may want to invite a team member or guest to speak who is knowledgeable about an issue.

To make the most of your meeting, take the time to gather any applicable information before the meeting takes place. Contact members who will be presenting beforehand and ask them to be prepared to present the information they have. Your proactive approach will save time, keep the meeting on track, and may prevent the need for an additional follow-up meeting.

STEP 3 | EXAMPLE

We shared our objectives with the participants when we issued the verbal invitations and asked them to bring their thoughts and ideas about branding the church. The agenda was simple: we needed to walk away from the meeting with a prioritized plan to deliver the marketing strategy with the best use of energy and budget. I gathered some branding samples and props I used in the business world.

| STEP 4: MAXIMIZE PREPARATION |

You have already determined your desired outcomes and objectives, so your next step is to prepare the agenda. You have a couple of options here. I highly recommend that you prepare the 3-D Outline™, which we discussed in detail in Chapter 3. You may want to prepare a separate agenda, or you may want this outline to double as your agenda. The agenda is a list of what you are going to cover. The 3-D Outline™ not only includes the *what*, but highlights the *why* and the *how* as well. Using the 3-D Outline™ as an agenda will help everyone see the times, what is going to be delivered and why, and who is going to present the information. The additional information on the outline lets your meeting members know that you have gone the extra mile in preparing. Your efforts will usually lead to better participation.

Let's take a look at a possible 3-D Outline™ for a quarterly staff meeting for all of your Sunday school teachers.

3-D OUTLINE™

Presentation Title:	Quarterly Sunday School Teachers' Meeting	Del. Date: 06/5
Audience:	All Sunday School Teachers	Start Time: 8:30 AM
Objectives:	• Provide fellowship time for teachers • Inspire vision • Preview curriculum for second quarter • Identify any issues in the department	End Time: 10:30 AM
Final Preparation Checklist:	[ ] Prepare agenda [ ] Ask teachers Jennifer T. and Amanda R. to relate stories of lives changed in their classes	[ ] Prepare slides of departmental goals [ ] Arrange for flip chart, DVD player

#	Time	What	Why	How	Who
1.	30	Continental Breakfast	Fellowship	Stand-up breakfast	All teachers
2.	5	Opening: • Prayer, Welcome • Review Objectives • Review Agenda	Gain buy-in	Speaking	Department head
3.	15	Review Sunday school goals and provide motivation and vision	Inspire vision	Slides, speaking, teacher testimonies	Teachers Jennifer T., Amanda R.
4.	30	Curriculum Preview: Video, review curriculum objectives, brief preview of each lesson	Preview curriculum	Video, discussion, flip chart to show flow of lessons	Department head, all teachers
5.	15	Small group discussion: Identify 3 things the department does well and 3 areas in need of improvement	Identify any issues in the department	Break-out session in groups of 5	All teachers
6.	15	Report outcomes of small groups and assign actions for improvement	Identify any issues in the department	Discussion, flip chart	All teachers, department head

#	Time	What	Why	How	Who
7.	10	Close: • Review action assignments • Encourage teachers to press toward the mark for the prize in their high calling • Prayer	Reinforce objectives	Speaking	Department head
	2 hrs.	**Total Time**			

Your meeting will likely run much smoother and be much more effective if you send the agenda and objectives (or the 3-D Outline™) to the participants a few days before the meeting. It eliminates surprises and gives your team members time to organize their thoughts about the agenda items and prepare for their participation.

Another big part of the preparation for a meeting is the room setup. The physical characteristics of a room can definitely have an impact on the meeting. Whenever possible, select a room that meets your needs. If you need to work within the constraints of an assigned meeting area, the following information will help you take full advantage of the way you set up the room.

George Lowe and I coauthored a book several years ago called *We've Got to Stop Meeting Like This,* which included several typical meeting room layouts, along with some of the characteristics, advantages, and limitations of each. The layouts also show the best places to put any flip charts, white boards, and screens. I have included a few of those layouts here that may be appropriate for meetings in a ministry setting.

WORKING WITH TYPICAL LAYOUTS

U-Shape

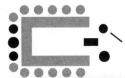

Characteristics	• Power resides at the head of the horseshoe. • Power differentials of the other positions are minimized. • Provides good focus on task. • Can be used for meetings with overhead or projected presentations and video conferencing arrangements.
Advantages	• Meeting leader can easiliy manage meeting behaviors of participants. • Sight lines are good at most positions. • High degree of interactivity is possible.
Limitations & Disadvantages	• Power at the head of the table can be used to draw focus. • Maximum group size for this layout is 25 to 30.

Semi-Circle (without table)

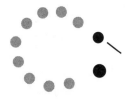

Characteristics	• Power resides in the center of the semi-circle. • Power differentials of the other positions are minimized. • Provides good focus on task.
Advantages	• Meeting leader can easiliy manage meeting behaviors of participants. • Sight lines are good at all positions. • High degree of interactivity is possible.
Limitations & Disadvantages	• Not good for meetings with overhead or projected presentations, or with extensive paper materials. • No place for coffee cups or juice glasses; note-taking must be done on laps. • Maximum group size for this layout is 10 to 15.

Truncated Oval with Presenter and Recorder

Characteristics	• Power resides at the head at the presenter position.
	• Power differentials of the other positions are minimized.
	• Provides good focus on task.
	• Can be used for meetings with overhead or projected presentations.
Advantages	• Meeting leader can easily manage meeting behaviors of participants.
	• Sight lines are good at most positions.
	• High degree of interactivity is possible.
Limitations & Disadvantages	• Power at the head of the table can be used to draw focus from the front of the room and the presenter.
	• Not suitable for video conferencing arrangements.
	• Maximum group size for this layout is 10 to 15.

Classroom

Characteristics	• Classic layout for informational presentations and training.
	• Power resides at the front of the room, but differentials of other participants are minimal.
	• Projected presentations are best, especially in larger rooms.
	• Some capability for interaction via Q & A.
Advantages	• Meeting leader can manage some behaviors of participants.
	• Forward looking sight lines are good at most positions.
	• Table space is available for coffee, juice, papers, and other meeting materials.
Limitations & Disadvantages	• Not suitable for video conferencing arrangements.
	• Limited interaction capability among participants.
	• Susceptible to inattention and side conversations.
	• Without unusual preparations, 50 to 60 is typically the maximum group size.

Roundtable

Characteristics	• Power resides where the ranking participant sits.
	• Power differentials among other seating positions are not substantial.
	• This layout provides for close and potentially intense interaction.
Advantages	• Sight lines are good at all positions.
	• Adequate space for coffee cups and juice glasses. Note-taking and paper handouts are not a problem.
Limitations & Disadvantages	• Not good for meetings with overhead or projected presentations.
	• Use of flip charts to record is limited.
	• Because a high degree of interactivity is possible, it brings with it the risk of higher levels of open conflict.
	• Group size for this layout is limited by the table; typically 12 to 24 max.

Small Theater Set-Up for Large Meeting Rooms

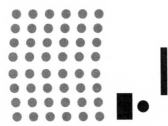

Characteristics	• Classic layout for larger informational presentations.
	• Power clearly resides at the front of the room.
	• Projected presentations are usually required.
	• Some capability for interaction and feedback to the presenter via Q & A if roving microphones are used.
Advantages	• Facilitator or meeting leader can manage some meeting behaviors of participants (for example, by choosing who to call on in Q & A) and controls the group via the power of the front of the room.
	• With proper planning, forward looking site lines are good at most positions—participants can see the presenter and presentation screen.

Limitations & Disadvantages	• Not suitable for video conferencing arrangements, unless the camera focuses soley on the presenter,
	• Flip charts don't work well for group memory.
	• No space for coffee and juice, papers, and other meeting materials.
	• Limited interaction capability among participants.
	• Need to use ushers or block back rows to assure filling the front rows first.
	• Maximum group size for this layout is largely dependent on the room size, type of projection, and screen size. With a single screen of ordinary size, the upper limit for this layout is 75-80.

Meeting rooms should match the size of your group as closely as possible. If you have to choose between two options that do not quite fit, meeting in a smaller room is often better than rattling around in wide-open spaces. If you are faced with a room that is too large, bring people together in one end or corner. Remember that environmental noise, coupled with poor acoustics, can be a major problem. If there is any doubt as to whether the speaker can be heard, use a PA system.

STEP 4 | EXAMPLE

We chose my studio for the meeting venue since it has all of the equipment in place to make the best use of meeting technology. We piped our objectives on the screen. As we moved through the brainstorming session, we had someone pipe the bullet lists of ideas and action items on the screen, and we developed a *Branding Matrix*.

| STEP 5: OPEN WELL |

If you want to open a meeting well, start on time. To establish a positive presence for a meeting, make certain you arrive early and begin on time. Your efforts communicate that you respect your meeting members' time and that you are ready to get to work. If you are participating rather than leading, arrive several minutes early to demonstrate that you are engaged and ready.

Once you welcome the group and make the necessary introductions, thank the participants for taking time from their busy schedules to attend. Then quickly recap the agenda. Even though you may have sent your agenda out ahead of time, it's a great idea to write your agenda items on a flip chart, white board, or chalkboard before the meeting. Mark an X by each item on the agenda as you complete it. This simple and unobtrusive technique will help volunteers keep track of your progress in the meeting and stay on task.

In your 3-D Outline™ you will have filled in the approximate times for each of the *what* segments. When you review the agenda with the participants, you may want to explain how much time you have allotted for each segment so everyone in the meeting can help you stay on schedule. If you go over your allotted time on one item, you can divide the remaining time among the remaining items and ask everyone to help you stay on track.

It is always good to establish meeting guidelines up front so participants know how and when they should respond. Should they hold their questions until the end or are you looking for continual feedback and interaction? Should they take notes? Should they offer up solutions as you go along? Your guidelines can be informal, or they can be written and distributed as a handout. You may just want to ask your participants to speak up if they have something they believe can be part of the solution. If you are pressed for time, you may want to have your participants write down their ideas and questions as you go through the briefing, and then have a discussion at the end. Setting good guidelines alleviates confusion, sets the tone for the meeting, increases confidence in your leadership, and allows you to accomplish your objectives.

STEP 5 | EXAMPLE

I thanked the participants for coming and sharing their expertise and ideas to promote the growth of the church. Then I reviewed the objectives and talked about our agenda item. Since it was a very casual meeting, the only guideline was to feel free to jump in with their brainstorming ideas.

| STEP 6: ENGAGE YOUR AUDIENCE |

Remember that it will take a team to achieve your objectives, and the synergy you create in the meeting can give you outstanding results. With few exceptions, the best solutions come from a focused group of people who are informed, involved, and engaged in the task. You can actually begin building involvement before the meeting. You can reap big dividends by ensuring that people who have a stake in the matter—or who know something about the issue—are brought into the discussion or presentation. All too often, work done in meetings is wasted because someone who had key information was not invited or consulted. If decisions need to be made, limit your meeting to the key stakeholders. Bringing in too many people who are not really essential to the process will likely bog down your meeting and frustrate participants.

To constantly keep people connected, use a variety of techniques that require participation. Brainstorming, breakout sessions, humor, and periodic process checks ("Are we on track?") create great opportunities for participant feedback. Be sure to thank participants for their active participation.

STEP 6 | EXAMPLE

Since this was a brainstorming session, everyone participated. There was a lot of synergy as we developed the *Branding Matrix* and discussed a variety of strategies for growing the church. We discussed several different branding tools that would get people out in the community talking about the church. One of my favorites was a business card with the next week's sermon topic that members could distribute in the community each week. I shared samples of some of the branding tools my clients use.

| STEP 7: CLOSE WITH ACTION |

If you have successfully achieved your objectives during the meeting, you will more than likely have assigned actions to various participants. It is very helpful to have someone taking notes and recording those actions. As you close your meeting, have your note taker review the action items to make sure everyone is clear on each action, its owner, and the timeframe to which they have committed. This strategy provides accountability for your group and a clear record of actions for you to use in tracking your progress. Within twenty-four hours after the meeting, send a quick e-mail to the participants to summarize agreements and action plans and to communicate results to those who were not in attendance. Be sure to thank the volunteers for their participation. That five-minute e-mail can prove invaluable toward achieving your objectives. At the beginning of the next meeting, you may want to preview the notes of the previous meeting to ensure that all of the actions have been handled.

STEP 7 | EXAMPLE

I closed the meeting by summarizing our action steps and making assignments for implementation. Then I thanked the participants again for coming and sharing their ideas.

Extraordinary meetings produce the extraordinary results you want to achieve when you are working for the Lord. Optimize your meetings and the use of your volunteers' time by using the information we have shared in this chapter. It may take some time, practice, and extra commitment on your part, but the results are worth it!

SCENARIO 6 VIP'S

! When people work together in meetings, the synergy that is produced can bring about positive results that could not be achieved by someone working alone.

! There are two main reasons why leaders do not conduct good meetings: they do not have good processes, or they procrastinate in their preparation.

! Your meeting will likely run much more smoothly and be more effective if you send the agenda and objectives (or the 3-D Outline™) to the participants a few days before the meeting.

! Meeting rooms should match the size of your group as closely as possible.

! Setting good guidelines alleviates confusion, sets the tone for the meeting, increases confidence in your leadership, and allows you to accomplish your objectives.

! With few exceptions, the best solutions come from a focused group of people who are informed, involved, and engaged in the task.

! As you close your meeting, have your note taker review the action items to make sure everyone is clear on each action, its owner, and the timeframe to which they have committed.

10. Wikipedia, wikipedia.org, http://en.wikipedia.org/wiki/Synergy (accessed September 30, 2008)

INTERACT WITH THE MEDIA

If it is possible, as far as it depends on you, live at peace with everyone.

—ROMANS 12:18

I t is inevitable that when you reach out to the community around you, regardless of the scale, you will encounter inquiring minds from the media and everyday people [who] want to know what your church is really about.

"The most important thing to realize is that you cannot control other people's thoughts and perceptions, but you can do your very best to be organized and prepared.

"So what does Public Relations, or PR, mean to your church?

"It means that the media can be a powerful tool to educate, promote and evangelize through your church's ministry and events.

"Being able to spread [God's] Word and reach out to people [who] do not yet have a personal relationship with Jesus Christ requires outreach, education and awareness of the good in Christianity, as seen through your church community." [11]

This quote from Spiritual Compass Marketing's Web site communicates the essence of this chapter. The media provides an unprecedented opportunity for you to demonstrate "awareness of the good in Christianity, as seen through your church community." Isn't promoting that awareness the underlying objective your church has any time it interacts with the media?

In Chapter 1 we talked about the power of negative communication in our media-driven world. Your church has an opportunity to counter negative representations of Christ and his church by putting out positive communication that confirms to the community around you that you are about *good*. You want *good* for people, and you want *good* for your community. Promoting such awareness to "inquiring minds" can lead to greater opportunities in the community, church growth, and evangelism.

Almost any proactive news that your church has to share benefits your community. Upcoming events, an exciting addition to your church, or even news about a new pastor or staff person provide a real benefit to your community. If it improves your church, it furthers your ability to reach out and minister to those in your community. You can use the media as a tool to help you accomplish that goal.

There may be other times when you must respond reactively to the news media, though I hope those are few and far between. Your church might be in a crisis situation or someone connected with your church may have done or said something inappropriate or even illegal. It's certainly not enjoyable working with the media in these situations. Your media strategy and approach for such difficulties, however, can have a tremendous impact on how your church or ministry weathers the storm. Handling a crisis situation well could positively impact your community's awareness of the good in Christianity.

Begin by preparing a media policy for your church that covers both proactive and reactive scenarios. A media policy addresses the six basic questions: who? what? where? when? why? and how? Who will be the official spokesperson? Oftentimes, the minister fills that role, but an articulate person within the congregation can also serve as the spokesperson. What protocols will govern the process? Where and when will the spokesperson be available to the media? Why is it a newsworthy event and why does the community care? How will you communicate the details for proactive and reactive media situations?

Be sure everyone on your church staff knows your media policy and is responsible to adhere to it. If possible, bring someone in to conduct media training for your spokespeople at least once a year. This training should include both content and technique in media communication.

Keep in mind that interactions with the media could include more than press releases and announcements. They could also take the form of advertising, feature articles, or letters to the editor on behalf of your congregation. Your congregation may want to applaud the efforts of your city council or mayor for initiating a project that will benefit the community. You might want to show your support for another nonprofit organization that has announced plans for a family-friendly program. These nontraditional media efforts can help your church promote awareness of the good in Christianity.

Remember that news is . . . well . . . news. Reporters look for things that create curiosity and excitement. Good or bad, that's the reality. Reporters are trained to pursue interesting stories, and that's what their jobs require of them. Even if your church's proactive news may not always seem interesting or exciting, do not let that stop you from releasing information that you think will benefit the community. If you have a new facility or are beginning an expansion, you have news the community can be proud of. The jobs created by the construction project could have a positive economic impact on the community. If you're holding an event, you are providing an opportunity for a family-friendly experience, and you are releasing information about something that may benefit other churches in the community. Be sure to think through any negatives that could be perceived from your release and counter them by highlighting as many positives as you can.

The information you find in this chapter will help you organize and prepare for proactive scenarios. For information on crisis communication, go to our Web site at www.purposefilledpresentations.com. I will show you the best way to deliver your message to the media, using an announcement about an exciting concert that your church is hosting as an example. Now let's apply the *Seven Steps to Effective Presentations* to your media announcement.

| STEP 1: CLARIFY OBJECTIVES |

We have already established promoting awareness of the good in Christianity as a possible overlying objective for your communication. Beyond that, your objective for releasing information about the concert will probably be to make the community aware of something good that is happening in your church. The youth in your community may be particularly excited about the concert, or a well-know artist that appeals to both youth and adults may be coming to your church. Include as many positive aspects of the event as you can to broaden the event's appeal to the people in your community.

STEP 1 | EXAMPLE

Larger churches often have a person on staff who handles media relations, whereas smaller churches more often designate an articulate volunteer who has some experience in that area, especially for dealing with proactive news. Our example story comes from a large church in east Texas, where Ken's role as a member of the pastoral staff includes interacting with the media. "We often use the media to proactively communicate to the community what we are going to be doing," Ken said. "Because ours is such a large church and our facilities are such a significant portion of our neighborhood, we like to keep our neighbors informed."

Ken told of an incident that happened a couple of years ago that demonstrated how his church used the media to relate the value it places on maintaining good relationships with its neighbors. "We were contemplating closing one of the streets on campus as part of a construction project," he said. "Our neighbors were worried that this would disrupt their normal travel routes and routines. Once we became aware of their concerns, we issued a press release to the media explaining that we had changed our plans in order to honor the needs of our neighbors. We realized that our responsibility was not only to be as effective and efficient as we could be economically with our facilities, but to value the relationships with the people around us as well."

The church is currently constructing two new buildings, both around 150,000 square feet. When they were far enough into the planning stage to know what they would be doing, Ken issued a news release to the community through the local media. He also sent more detailed information about the project, including pictures and graphics, and invited the media representatives to the groundbreaking ceremony. His objectives were twofold: 1) to make the community aware of the project itself and how it would affect travel routes, and 2) to remind the community that the church was a vital and viable part of the community and, as such, was creating more room for the people to come and be a part of what was going on there.

"When we enter into a construction project," Ken explained, "our primary focus is to provide a facility that not only benefits us as a church, but one that also benefits the community at large." As an example, he said the church would soon start construction on a conference center—one that would probably be the only facility of its kind in east Texas. It will house two thousand people for a conference and fourteen hundred people for a sit-down dinner. "A lot of groups here are looking for that sort of thing," he said, "so we're trying to make them aware that we are not just growing for our benefit, but for the benefit of the community as well."

| STEP 2: DEFINE YOUR AUDIENCE |

Anytime you interact with the media, you have two audiences: the reporters and their readers, viewers, or listeners. Your interaction with the reporters will probably affect the quality or tone of the message that reaches their audiences. Maintain an updated list of local media that includes reporters' names, addresses, e-mail, telephone numbers, and fax numbers. *Then make friends in the media.* Your media relations should be very positive. Even though your news may not seem as controversial and exciting as some reporters may like, the genuine and friendly relationships you pursue with them on an individual basis should impact their personal awareness of the good in Christianity. Positive relationships pay off when reporters understand and have good feelings about your church.

If you will be doing a personal interview about an event, gather information about the interviewer ahead of time. Know your host's name so you can use it once or twice during the course of the interview. Think about the reporter's motivation for running this particular story. Does she have experience reporting on Christian concerts or other community happenings? Can you find some of her previous articles or broadcasts to see what sort of information she may be looking for?

It is very helpful to understand the diverse motivations and methods of reporters from the various media outlets. While you may work with Internet-based media such as blogs, podcasts, or e-zines, the principles for working with traditional media apply. The primary difference is that Internet-based releases and interviews may remain in circulation or readily accessible archives for longer periods of time.

When you are working with radio or podcast reporters, keep in mind that they usually:

! Are very low-key [12]
! Want taped interviews

! Will run one to two minute stories
! Want a good ten-second sound bite for news feeds to affiliates
! Can reach the public quickly

Television reporters, in general:

! Want personal interviews
! May spend a few minutes off camera with you preparing for the inter-
view and putting you at ease
! Will use ten to twenty second sound bites, even though the on-camera
session may last for ten minutes
! Need visuals of people doing interesting things
! May run the story live, but usually record and edit into two-minute segments
! Have mid-afternoon deadlines for evening news
! Often simplify complex issues

Newspaper and e-zine reporters usually:

! Conduct interviews by telephone or e-mail
! Conduct interviews that are longer than TV or radio interviews
! Write down as much as they can of what you say
! Look for interesting metaphors, similes, characterizations, colorful
terms, or inconsistencies
! Deal with more complex issues
! Will often do advance stories
! Offer possible coverage in multiple sections [13]

Your ultimate audience, of course, is the people you want to reach through whatever media venue you are working with. It's important to know as much as you can about that audience. If you're working with a radio station, for example, find out about its listener profile. How many people does the media outlet reach? You can usually find how many subscribers a newspaper or magazine has by researching the published information for advertisers. While wattage does not always reveal a radio station's reach, radio stations that broadcast at less than 25,000 watts are usually considered small. Consider the different socio-economic and age groups that each outlet reaches. Think through how you want to impact the audience with your news story.

Since the work and distinctions for the next two steps run together while working with the media, we are going to address them together.

STEP 2 | EXAMPLE

"Actually, we have three audiences when we communicate through the media," Ken said. "We have fourteen thousand members in our church, which amounts to approximately one-eighth of our community. Because our membership comprises such a large portion of our community, we not only communicate to the reporters themselves and the community at large, but we communicate to our membership through the media as well. We couch our media messages in terms of those three audiences.

"We understand that many reporters do not understand what our purpose is and what we are all about, so for that audience we find that we need to define our language in most of our communication with them. We do not assume that they know what we are talking about."

Ken and his staff have established good working relationships with the media. "We use primarily newspaper and television media," he said. "We are in a relatively small television market, and there is a lot of turnover among the reporters. Most of the anchor people are pretty consistent, and we have their personal e-mail addresses. So we send press releases to them personally as well as to the media outlets in general."

| STEP 3: GATHER CONTENT & STEP 4: MAXIMIZE PREPARATION |

As you prepare for the interview, pull together all of your resources. Have you done a press release? If so, highlight information on the press release and have it in front of you. If there is a committee or group of people that is handling the concert, make sure you ask its members what aspects of the concert you should promote. Get quotes and key details if appropriate. Take plenty of notes and organize them into a format that will make them easy to use in your interview.

Several years ago, a friend and coauthor, Kim Dower, and I put together a piece called *Maximize Your Media Presentations: Great Tips for Dealing with the Media.* Here are some tips from that piece that may be helpful as you gather your content and prepare for your interview:

! Form a team of trusted advisors to help you focus on the news event and the appropriate responses to any questions likely to be asked.

! Brainstorm the questions. Put yourself in the shoes of the interviewer. Ask yourself the "who, what, and why" of the news event.

! Do not skip over questions that you do not really have great data or answers for in hopes that they will not get asked. You will likely have to answer these difficult questions at some point. Prepare yourself now.

! Go beyond the basics. Think of everything else you might want to know if you were affected by the news.

! Give the interviewer something he thinks he wants. Make it a very positive story and show how it will positively impact the community.

! Good reporters are looking for information that is clear, concise, conversational, catchy and colorful. Following this simple guideline while conveying the message you want to share will help get you heard.

! Gather intelligence before the interview. Find out the reporter's understanding of the exact nature of her assignment, when the story will run, how much time or space the story will be given, any research that has already been done on the story, and any other people being interviewed for the story.

! Make your answers fit the format of the venue and work with the tone of the venue. For example, if you are interviewing for a story for your local newspaper, your answers will be different than if you are interviewing for a local talk show that has a humorous side.

! Know your key points so you can make those points no matter what else is asked.

! If your story involves more than one interview, you will have heard ninety percent of the questions you will be asked after the first two or three interviews. Develop a sharply drawn, clearly thought-out, fully articulated response for each question. Do not start making up totally new responses when you already have good ones at your command.

! Remember that the reporter does interviews for a living, and you are an amateur. So practice, practice, practice. Practice each answer until it sounds natural and can be delivered with conviction and sincerity.

STEPS 3 & 4 | EXAMPLE

"When we are communicating with the media about a construction project," Ken said, "we boil down the facts and decide what would be of the greatest interest to the community. So we get information from our architects, from our builders, and from the building committee. But we also get information internally from our staff, because we want to communicate that this is not just a building—it represents ministry. We talk to the people in charge of the ministries that will be affected, whether it is our children's ministry, our adult education ministry, or whatever, and personalize our news releases to relate to the people we will be ministering to.

"When we prepare a press release, we often do it in the format of a series of quotations, usually by our pastor. That way, the reporters can use the press release almost as if it were an interview with the pastor. We have found that they actually pick up on our news a lot faster that way than if we just send them a lot of facts about what we are doing. If you couch your facts in a quotation from the pastor, that puts them at a whole different level."

PREPARING A PRESS RELEASE

! Allow enough time for the press to respond to your announcement and prepare for your event. Mail news releases at least two weeks before the event.
! State your message simply without Christian or technical jargon.
! Make sure to include vital information such as the time, place, and location of the event. Include the name of a contact person with a phone number and e-mail address.
! Clearly state the sponsor of the event and those who will benefit from it.
! Show the costs of the event, if any, and give information about who may attend.

! Double-check phone numbers, the spelling of people's names, and the listed dates and times.

! Keep it short, use wide margins, and double-space the text.

! Proofread the news release carefully, and ask someone else to look it over for you to make sure the information is complete and makes sense.

! Make sure that the contact person listed on the news release is aware that his or her name and phone number are being provided to the press.

! Make sure your church's full name and address, phone, fax, and e-mail are clearly identified.

! Give a quick overview of your church history somewhere in the news release. This is often included in the concluding paragraph.

! Make sure that each envelope has the correct name and address of the media contact, and that it includes an accurate return address.

| STEP 5: OPEN WELL |

It is always good to establish rapport with your interviewers. If the interviewer allows, get into some light conversation to help warm you up. Use this time to gather some information about the interviewer. Asking a few questions in the beginning may help you steer the interview. You might ask how the interviewer will use the information, when it might run, and what he is hoping to accomplish during the interview.

Make sure you put the emphasis and strong points of your story right up front. You do not always have the option of directing your own opening, but have that in mind in case the option presents itself.

STEP 5 | EXAMPLE

"About ninety-five percent of our interviews are just answering reporters' questions," Ken told us. "Often when they ask questions, though, we respond in such a way that we lead the reporters in the direction we really want them to go. Since they like to use sound bites from our responses, the first bit of information we give is usually a short snippet that can be used in its entirety and that contains all the important facts in a nutshell. If we respond in a long diatribe, we know they will edit it down and will often take it out of context."

"I do like to establish rapport with the reporter before the interview," Ken continued. "In fact, when a television reporter comes on campus, I make it a point to meet both the reporter and the cameraman. I like to make it personal for the cameraman and acknowledge him and his contribution, because he often has as much to do with the outcome of the story as the reporter does."

STEP 6: ENGAGE YOUR AUDIENCE

Engaging your audience during an interview requires some unique strategies and guidelines. For example, you should be wary of using sarcasm or jokes during an interview as the reporter can take sound bites from your time together that may not reflect your intentions. The following standard rules and tips, taken from my *Maximize Your Media Presentations: Great Tips for Dealing with the Media,* will help you engage the interviewer and the audience during your interview:

! Dress appropriately. Neatness counts, so be sure to be as well groomed as possible.
! Ascertain from the reporter if the interview is live, recorded, or both.
! Respect the microphone, but let the reporter control it. He or she will place it where it needs to be.
! Always remember that any microphone may be live at any time and capable of transmitting your voice.
! Be cognizant of your surroundings. The environment in which you hold your interview can optimize the impact of your message.
! Be approachable and conversational. Be yourself.
! Use the host's name once or twice during the course of the interview.
! Attend the interview with one central theme in mind. Repeat the theme often in a conversational tone.
! Make your key points, no matter what else is asked.
! When you do not know the answer, say, "I don't know." Then offer to get the information to the reporter immediately after the interview.
! Know the major points you want to make in the interview and make them in the course of answering the reporter's questions. Address your needs and the reporter's.
! Stick to the point and don't ramble.
! Pay attention. Keep your eyes on the interviewer. Do not look at the camera. It will find you.

❗ Relate to others by bringing the audience and interviewer into the questions and answers. Relate your responses with such phrases as "Many people have . . ." "I think most people have experienced . . ." or look at the interviewer and ask, "Have you ever . . . ?"

❗ Use humor. Do not tell jokes or use sarcasm, but do not be afraid to be amusing.

❗ Make your point, back it up with an example, and then make your point again.

❗ Characterize your answers. Some of your responses to the interviewer's questions should begin with phrases such as "The most interesting aspect" and "The most startling idea."

❗ Use vigorous language. Whenever appropriate, use dramatic words such as "passion" and "crucial."

❗ Do not say, "Well," "Uh" or "You know." It is much better to pause for a second and start with the idea than to begin with an empty phrase that turns your listener off.

❗ Use short anecdotes. When you have a short story that makes your point, use it.

❗ Avoid detailed answers. After thirty to forty-five seconds, the chances are you are speaking too much. Answer questions fully, but don't get bogged down in extended responses. If the interviewer wants to know more, she will ask you.

❗ Avoid offering a simple *yes* or *no*. There are more exciting words, such as "certainly," "absolutely," or "never" that convey greater conviction. Always explain the reasons for your answer.

Facing a news camera can be terrifying for many people. An otherwise calm and confident speaker may freeze up when he hears that the tape is rolling or that the live feed is ready to go. Unless your interviewer instructs you otherwise, block the camera out. Concentrate on talking with the reporter and stick to your talking points. Remember that God has given you the opportunity to help others see his goodness and the good in his church. God has promised to give you the words you will need when the time comes. As you prepare for your television or video interview, review the following tips on nonverbal communication with the media.

❗ Verbal and nonverbal messages must match. Verbal, vocal, and visual images must all be in sync.

❗ Most communication experts agree that anywhere from sixty-five to ninety percent of effectiveness in communication depends on nonverbal messages.

! An interviewee who fears facing a camera will have great trouble conveying his message. Energy, animation, and enthusiasm are essential to a successful on-camera interview.

! Convey three essential nonverbal elements:

- Openness—be happy to talk
- Concern—care about the outcome
- Authority—project a self-confident air of knowing what you are talking about

! Facial expressions should welcome the viewer into your environment.

! Make sure your smile is authentic and genuine.

! Be careful not to stand so that the sun is directly in your eyes. If you are in a position that requires you to squint to see, politely ask to be moved.

! For tense or serious situations, do not frown. Instead, practice facial expressions that convey sincere concern.

! Maintain eye contact with your interviewer. It is perfectly acceptable to look away occasionally, but do not overdo it. Avoiding eye contact will make you appear shifty or as if you are in over your head.

! If it is a television interview, avoid nodding or shaking your head. These movements appear exaggerated on camera.

! Use gestures when speaking. They add sincerity and warmth to your words.

! Do not clasp your hands behind you or put them in your pockets.

! When sitting during an interview, sit erect and lean slightly forward. This posture will help you look eager and interested in the events around you.

! Do not expect the interviewer or camera crew to tell you that your hair is out of place or that you have spinach between your teeth. Check yourself thoroughly in a mirror before going on camera.

Step 6 | EXAMPLE

"We have several locations here that we know work well for interviews," Ken said, "particularly for television interviews. So I enjoy taking our television reporters to a place on campus that works well for their shots.

"Reporters usually like facts rather than application, so I do not usually steer the interview in that direction. Sometimes if it gets too personal, it gets cut.

"I think another way we engage our audience is by being ourselves. We train our pastors not to attempt to live up to an image while they are on camera. We tell them, 'There is nothing worse than an interview with a pastor who sounds like a pastor. Just be yourself—be a human being.'"

NEWS CONFERENCES

News conferences, when presented properly, give reporters everything they need to write the story you want. But be careful to only call a news conference when there is real news to cover that all media will deem important. If you call conferences for stories that are not real news, you may not have anyone to report to at your conference, and media outlets will be less likely to pay attention to your church for future releases or conferences. Remember the following principles and practices when you hold a news conference:

! For a news conference, you have no control over which reporter will cover a story. If you phone the interviewer directly, you control who asks the questions.

! Choose the appropriate venue to hold the news conference. A well-placed banner in the background or a view of the church adds emphasis to the conference.

! Make sure each person selected to comment at the news conference has something important to say and is prepared to say it.

! Each person at the news conference should be properly attired to convey his or her message. Do not overdress for a more casual situation.

! Rehearse with all members of the team who will present at the conference. Have an audience who asks questions so that they can prepare their answers and experience thinking on their feet.

❗ Answers to expected questions should be formulated and rehearsed, yet delivered in a conversational tone. Do not overact.

❗ Help team members remember to take a breath and think about answers to questions they may be surprised to hear.

❗ Make sure that each team member knows who should answer which question. Team members should feel comfortable handing off a question to another member of the team who has more expertise on a particular subject.

❗ The earlier in the day you call a news conference, the more attention it is likely to get. Conferences called later in the afternoon rush news deadlines and may be hastily put together or cut altogether at the studio.

❗ After the news conference, do not leave too soon. Knowledgeable news reporters may want a moment of your time so they do not have to ask their key questions in front of their competitors. Give reporters a chance to help further the message you want conveyed.

| STEP 7: CLOSE WITH ACTION |

If given the opportunity, summarize your points briefly at the end of an interview (or at the end of a lengthy response if the interview is long). Refocus the listener's attention with such phrases as "The most important thing to remember . . ." or "The point I would like you to carry away from all this is . . ."

Remember your objectives, and ask the reporter to help you get your communication out to the community. You might ask if there is any other information you can furnish, like a program or a poster. Be sure to thank the reporter for the interview. If you have found common ground in your information-gathering stage, your closing moments with the reporter may be a good time to bring it up. You may want to compliment her on a recent story and tell her you are looking forward to reading or hearing the one she will be writing for your church. Continually look for ways to build positive relations.

Step 7 | EXAMPLE

"We approach all reporters as if they were potential church members," Ken said. "They live in our community, so that's a possibility. They have the same needs as other people, and sometimes more since they can be somewhat isolated because of their jobs. So when they leave, we make a point to welcome them back without the camera to just enjoy what we have to offer. I add another little touch, as well. After the feature story runs, I send a note to the reporter telling him or her how well I thought it was handled and how much we appreciate the story. That often encourages the reporter to come back without the camera."

May all of your media relations be good! Remember, you not only represent your church to your community, you are Christ's ambassador as well.

SCENARIO 7 VIP'S

! The media provides an unprecedented opportunity for you to demonstrate "awareness of the good in Christianity, as seen through your church community."

! Almost any proactive news that your church has to share benefits your community. If it improves your church, it furthers your ability to reach out and minister to those in your community.

! Prepare a media policy for your church that covers both proactive and reactive scenarios.

! Any time you interact with the media, you have two audiences: the reporters and their readers, viewers, or listeners. Your interaction with the reporters will probably affect the quality or tone of the message that reaches their audiences.

! Your ultimate audience is the people you want to reach through whatever media venue you are working with. It's important to know as much as you can about that audience.

! Make friends in the media.

! In an interview, make sure you put the emphasis and strong points of your story right up front in case you have the option of directing your own opening.

❗ If given the opportunity, summarize your points briefly at the end of an interview.

11. Spiritualcompassmarketing.com, http://www.spiritualcompassmarketing.com/church_event_christian_marketing_PR_public_relations_event_promotion_ministry.html (accessed October 27, 2008).

12. Information in this section was taken from the National Conference of State Legislators' Web site, http://www.ncsl.org/programs/nlpes/training/fallconf/pds01/janbush/index.htm (accessed October 27, 2008).

13. Information in this section was taken from "Interacting Constructively with the Media," Belinda Willis, Texas Municipal League, http://www.tml.org/2008ElectedOfficials/July-InteractingwithMediaConstructively.pdf (accessed October 27, 2008).

REACH OUT TO OTHERS

> Then the King will say to those on his right, 'Come, you who are blessed by my Father; take your inheritance, the kingdom prepared for you since the creation of the world. For I was hungry and you gave me something to eat, I was thirsty and you gave me something to drink, I was a stranger and you invited me in, I needed clothes and you clothed me, I was sick and you looked after me, I was in prison and you came to visit me.

> **—MATTHEW 25:34-36**

There are two extreme camps of thought in the church when it comes to outreach. The first camp believes that our message is so vitally important that we should use whatever means necessary to bring others to Christ. The other camp has nearly forsaken the idea of reaching out to others with the *message* of the gospel and has chosen to only meet real and practical needs of this world such as hunger and shelter. Scriptural outreach brings the two camps together. The message of salvation through Jesus is *the* most important news anyone can ever hear. And one of the most effective ways of sharing that message is by meeting the practical needs of those we want to reach.

Jesus spent his entire earthly ministry modeling a life of servanthood for us. He, who held all power and authority in Heaven and on earth, "did not come to be served, but to serve, and to give his life as a ransom for many" (Matthew 20:28). And Jesus told us in Matthew 20:26, that "whoever wants to become great among you must be your servant." Servant evangelism gained serious traction in the American church nearly 30 years ago. Leaders such as Steve Sjogern built megachurches and reached cities by sharing God's love with people in practical ways. A related term is "outward living." The heart of outward living is to live in sync with the teachings of Jesus and focus outward on the needs of others.

Many churches today are combining the *call* to share the message of Christ with the *action* of meeting practical and real needs. Outreach is moving to the top of the priority list, servant evangelism is on the rise, and entire churches are getting involved in outreach experiences.

Your church may be planning a summer of service where its people will help the aged, ill, or underprivileged with lawn work, repairs, groceries, or errands. Or perhaps you are doing a season of service covering the Thanksgiving and Christmas holidays, making sure the needy in your community are blessed with holiday food and gifts.

Some churches are initiating outreach to other populations in their communities. Maybe your church is organizing workers to hand out bottles of water at a Fourth of July event or to give away free nachos and water at a street festival. Perhaps your youth are doing a free car wash in the community. I have been involved in events in which churches asked me to provide free presentation seminars so they could reach out to unchurched business people in their communities. Still others initiate relationship-building ministries or events that reach out to unchurched neighbors.

Whatever the venue, there is a widespread energy toward outreach. And every outreach event involves some type of presentation to those being served, whether it lasts for a few seconds, a few minutes, or is ongoing through the relationships that develop. Whether you are leading a servant evangelism effort in your church or are reaching out to your neighbors, the thoughts and ideas we share in this chapter will help you in your ministry efforts.

SADDLEBACK CHURCH IN CALIFORNIA: A MODEL FOR OUTREACH

In our research for this chapter, we talked with Jeremiah Goley, a pastor on the missions staff at Saddleback Church. He shared with us that outreach is a major component of Saddleback's mission. The church is unique in that it places a high priority on equipping *all* of its members to live a mission-oriented life that communicates with others the message of Jesus.

The church has integrated a strategic discipleship process for its members, composed of four classes. The last class, which they call "Class 401: Discovering Your Life Mission," is described as the church's "sharing your faith class." In the first part of that class, members learn what God's mission is for the world and discover what their role is within that mission. They learn what the gospel of Christ is and the significance of the cross of Christ. They discuss the problem (in a world that largely does not know Christ) and the solution. In the second segment of Class 401, members learn how to share the story of what Christ has done in their lives. In the third part, they learn of local and global opportunities for them to get involved and live out their life mission.

In Class 401, members are not taught *what* to say to those with whom they share the message of Christ. Rather, they are given tools to teach them *how* to communicate in their unique ways, using what God has done in their lives and the transformation that has resulted. They are taught that being a voice for Christ is most effective in the context of relationships, for it is in relationships that the love and hope of Jesus is encountered. They focus on growing lifestyles that will overflow with that message.

As a church, Saddleback is always looking for ways to build those relationships with the people who live in the surrounding communities. Recently that has taken the form of civil forums, in which the church invites world leaders in the areas of science, business, education, art, entertainment, government, health, and religion to come to the church and talk about their areas of expertise. The topics of conversation are chosen to serve a particular need or area of interest for the surrounding communities.

At any given time, there are approximately thirty local organized outreach opportunities for the members of Saddleback to participate in. Those opportunities may involve reaching out to the elderly, the homeless, those in poverty, or military families, or they may be after-school programs for children. Saddleback members are even encouraged and coached in creating their own local outreach opportunities. Because the message is continually reinforced at Saddleback that its members have a lot that God can use to spread the love of Christ, they eagerly participate. In 2007 there were over twenty thousand people who participated in various local outreaches.

| STEP 1: CLARIFY OBJECTIVES |

There are varying approaches to the actual presentation that takes place in a servant evangelism event. Though most agree that the ultimate objective of any outreach event is to give people the opportunity to start following Christ, some churches offer a presentation of the message of the gospel to every participant in the event. They train their people to look for ways to connect as they are meeting the needs of those they are serving. The connection often takes place through casual conversation, during which the person shares his story about what Christ has done in his life.

In another approach the objective is to simply allow the recipients to see and experience the love of God in a tangible way. The church members conducting the outreach do not force a conversation. Rather, they let the Holy Spirit do the speaking. The idea is that as the people serve, God's Spirit will do the heart work. That is not to say that the gospel message is never presented in this scenario. Most churches encourage their workers to be sensitive to the opportunity if the recipient is open or actively seeking answers.

Whether you are looking to give a presentation of the gospel or if you just want to serve people in the way that Jesus taught and modeled, clarifying your objectives will make your efforts much more meaningful and effective.

STEP 1 | EXAMPLE

The church in our example is planning an event that it calls "Share the Warmth." The church newsletter describes the event: "We are seeking to serve homeowners who are physically or financially limited and are unable to care for the winterization of their own homes. Homeowners will be recommended through individuals or partnerships with existing community organizations."

According to a member of the team, their overall objective is to show the love of God in a tangible way, letting their serving do the talking. The newsletter describes their service objective like this: "Community Impact is about meeting the practical needs of the people in our communities. We believe that there are plenty of folks in our communities who will need help staying warm this winter. We want to help."

| STEP 2: DEFINING YOUR AUDIENCE |

Obviously, your audience in an outreach scenario is going to be the people you are serving. The possible audiences are endless. You may be serving the underprivileged, the elderly, children, college students, military families, or countless other groups who have real needs. Begin by thinking about the group you are trying to reach. You and your group will likely meet practical needs. As you prepare your outreach and presentation, think through their emotional and spiritual needs as well.

STEP 2 | EXAMPLE

The church defined the audience for its outreach as "homeowners who are physically or financially limited and are unable to care for the winterization of their own homes." They found that many who fit those qualifications were seniors, shut-ins, and single moms. As they prepared to meet their audience members' physical needs, they prayerfully considered how to meet their emotional and spiritual needs as well.

| STEP 3: GATHER CONTENT |

Your church's outreach team leader may give you direction on the content of your presentation, your small group may work together to decide how you want to reach out, or you may lead the charge. Your objectives will guide the type of content you need to gather. If your group will be presenting the gospel message, some members will likely need training.

If your team is new to this sort of outreach, you may want to talk to others who have done the same kind of ministry. You can find tips on servant evangelism at *www.servantevangelism.com*. Your whole church or small group can go through outreach training through programs such as Steve Sjogren's *Outflow* or Bill Hybles' *Just Walk Across the Room*.

Step 3 | EXAMPLE

Our example church provided guidelines for the spoken presentation and the service interaction through various media: announcements, the weekly newsletter, mass e-mails, and phone calls. Their newsletter also provided the following information on the service interaction: "Teams of six to ten people will be working together to complete typical winterization projects. These may include covering windows with plastic, installing storm windows, cleaning windows, caulking, weather stripping, raking, gutter cleaning, installing smoke detector batteries, and replacing outside lights. Each homeowner will be contacted prior to 'Share the Warmth' to confirm exactly what is to be done at their home."

| Step 4: Maximize Preparation |

Though there may be dozens or even hundreds of things to do to prepare for the actual execution of your church's outreach event, we will address only those that pertain to your presentation.

Your outreach team leader may have given you training, guidelines, and perhaps even suggestions for your interaction with the recipient, but you probably were not given a script. Prayerfully think through all of the information you have been given, asking God to prepare your heart and to give you right responses to recipients' questions. Pray that God will compel the people you interact with to hear more about why you are serving. You want to be able to meet spiritual needs if the opportunity arises, and that can only be done with God working through you.

You may want to turn some of your unknowns into knowns by going to the place where you will be serving and getting comfortable with the environment. If you will be serving at a big event, see where your team will set up. Check the weather to see how to dress. And gather necessary tools, supplies, or food well in advance so you do not feel the pressure of procrastination.

Since the actual interaction in an outreach scenario is often either less than a minute long or involves an extended conversation, it would be best to concentrate on the global objective versus preparing a 3-D Outline™. Remember that your ultimate objectives are to offer people the opportunity to start following Christ and to allow the recipients to see and experience the love of God. Be ready to share your testimony if you have the opportunity. It would be a great idea to read Scenario Chapter 1 of this book (Share Your Testimony) as you prepare for your outreach event.

STEP 4 | EXAMPLE

The person directing the outreach at our primary example church shared with me that she met with her team leaders the week before the outreach event. They reviewed the physical skills needed to do the work and discussed ways to interact with the homeowners. A member of their team had volunteered for Habitat for Humanity, so they capitalized on his experience. Since their event required tools, their newsletter asked team members for help in the following way: The church "will provide all of the materials needed to winterize (plastic, caulk, light bulbs, batteries, leaf bags). Each team will be asked to bring their own rakes, ladders, work gloves, and other tools needed. A complete list will be provided to team leaders, who will then coordinate their team's supplies."

The director asked her troops to assemble early on the day of the activity, and they reviewed the expectations for the day. She reminded them that their primary jobs were to make the homeowners feel cared for. She asked them to pay special attention to the homeowners and to use common sense in both their work and their interactions. At least one person on each team was designated to do nothing but chat with the homeowner while the rest of the team did the physical work.

| STEP 5: OPEN WELL |

During any outreach the first thing to do is warmly greet the people you are serving. Let your body language, your tone, and your words convey the real reason you are there: to show the love of God. Let the joy in your voice match the joy in your heart (or vice versa, if need be). You may only have a few seconds to reach your objective, so start with the end in mind!

STEP 5 | EXAMPLE

Team leaders called before the outreach event and introduced themselves to the homeowners. When they arrived, they warmly greeted the homeowners and introduced themselves and their teams before starting to work.

| STEP 6: ENGAGE YOUR AUDIENCE |

Here is where you have an opportunity to follow Christ's direction in Matthew 5:16 to "let your light shine before men, that they may see your good deeds and praise your Father in heaven." Remember, everything you do and say represents God, so use the opportunity well. Inexperienced team members may huddle in groups with their friends and have little interaction with those they are serving—especially at the beginning of your event. That is a pretty good way to defeat your objectives.

You may have as little as fifteen seconds to interact with the person you are serving. If your team is handing out water or cold drinks at a festival or street event, for example, you may only have time to give them a warm smile and tell each person to have a good day. If you are taking food to someone and actually going into the home, you may have a minute or so. In any case, if they ask why you are doing what you are doing, your response could be one of the following:

❗ We are serving out of love for God and love for you.
❗ We just want to show you that God loves you.
❗ Jesus came to serve, and we want to be like Jesus.
❗ We are doing the good works that God has prepared us to do.
❗ God has asked me to love my neighbor. That's you.
❗ This is my small way to show you God's kindness.

Choose a couple of responses you are comfortable with and use them throughout the event. If you have more time to interact, ask questions to get a conversation going while you're working. Show recipients that you genuinely care by asking about their families. Let them tell their story. Treat them as you would anyone else with whom you want to establish a relationship. Some churches give out cards with information about the church. Your team leader may prefer to give cards to all of your recipients, or he may prefer that you only give them out if someone asks about your church. The information on the card varies as well. Some have only their Web address on the cards, while others give full information, including a map showing the location of the church.

STEP 6 | EXAMPLE

The person so designated spent the entire time visiting with the homeowner while the rest of the team did the physical work. As instructed, that person followed the homeowner's lead in the conversation. If it drifted to spiritual matters, that was good. But if it did not, that was all right, too. The main objective was to share the love of Jesus, which they expressed in their own words. They listened as the homeowners told of their lives and their families. Many reported very positive conversations that turned to spiritual matters, where the team members had a chance to talk about what God had done in their lives. Some homeowners were open to having the teams pray with them, but not all were interested.

| STEP 7: CLOSE WITH ACTION |

If you get an opportunity to close or wrap-up the interaction, perhaps you could arrange a time for follow-up. Or you might get a name, address, and phone number so you can follow up later with a letter, a card, or a phone call. You could even send a picture if you have a photographer on hand.

Some churches include follow-up in their objectives, and they put a high priority on building relationships with the people they serve. If your group has shared the gospel with the people you served, follow-up is essential—especially if someone has decided to follow Christ. Your church hopefully has a plan in place for follow-up ministry that includes getting that person plugged into a church, as well as discipleship and mentoring. If transportation is an issue, you may need to arrange for your church van to pick the person up or partner with others in your church to cover transportation.

STEP 7 | EXAMPLE

Our primary example church sent follow-up letters to the homeowners saying, "Thank you for allowing us to come. We hope it was a blessing to you." The letters went on to say that they would contact them the following winter if the church had the opportunity to assist them again. The church's contact information was on the letterhead, but they left any initiative to attend the church up to the homeowner.

SCENARIO 8 VIP'S

! Many churches today are combining the call to share the message of Christ with the action of meeting practical and real needs.

! Every outreach event involves some type of presentation to those being served, whether it lasts for a few seconds, a few minutes, or is ongoing through the relationships that develop.

! Whether you are looking to give a presentation of the gospel or if you just want to serve people in the way that Jesus taught and modeled, clarifying your objectives will make your efforts much more meaningful and effective.

! Be ready to share your testimony if you have the opportunity. (See Scenario Chapter 1: Share Your Testimony.)

! During any outreach the first thing to do is warmly greet the people you are serving. Let your body language, your tone, and your words convey the real reason you are there: to show the love of God.

! Remember, everything you do and say represents God, so use the opportunity well.

! If your group has shared the gospel with the people you served, follow-up is essential—especially if someone has decided to follow Christ.

CREATE GREAT FIRST IMPRESSIONS

> Offer hospitality to one another without grumbling. Each one should use whatever gift he has received to serve others, faithfully administering God's grace in its various forms.

—1 PETER 4:9, 10

For the children of God, hospitality should be an overflow of the love and grace we have ourselves experienced. More than any other place, hospitality should be evident in the church—where people worship and serve the God whose entire essence is love for those he created. The heart and attitude of a church is displayed in the way its people connect with each other and with guests.

Hopefully, the people at your church are like family to you. I hope you feel eager to see them every week, and that you have experienced the joy and depth of relationship Paul describes in 1 Thessalonians 2:8, where he says they shared "not only the gospel of God but our lives as well." Just as someone who is newly married hopes and expects to be quickly integrated into the family system, most guests who visit a church desire to find the warmth and acceptance associated with connection to a family. Guests will quickly decide if there is any hope for being welcomed as family through the first impression they receive.

To put it another way, the church should be the ultimate host. When guests come to our homes, we make them feel comfortable. We invite them in. We ask them to sit down. We offer them something to drink. We turn off the TV, and we give them our full attention. We put them at ease and make them feel important.

Guests who come to the house of God should be given the same care. We have the chance to offer them warmth and hospitality in exchange for the anxieties and uncertainties they have about visiting. For all who are involved in the "first impression" ministry, the comfort level of guests should be foremost in their minds.

In many churches, a guest could encounter at least six or seven personal touches or connections during the course of his visit and the two or three days following from:

❗ Parking attendants
❗ Greeters
❗ Information table attendants
❗ Coffee bar hosts
❗ Ushers
❗ Follow-up hosts

If you are involved in any of these positions in your church, your role is crucial. Every position within a first impressions ministry affords an opportunity to present the pulse of the entire organization. Your first impressions team is the face of your ministry to visitors, and it serves as a representative of Christ to those who do not yet know him. You may be one of the first faces guests see, and you have the awesome opportunity to make a first impression that reflects your church and your Lord. What a privilege and responsibility!

I recently connected with a church consultant by the name of Thomas Harrison. Reverend Harrison sometimes conducts "mystery-worshipper" surveys to evaluate churches on things like hospitality and cleanliness, appearance, and the worship experience. His surveys help churches be their best by making a good first impression. Reverend Harrison told me that guests look for four things when they visit a church:

❗ Warmth
❗ Genuineness
❗ Friendliness
❗ An encounter with God

I asked Reverend Harrison for his advice for this chapter, and this is what he wrote:

Tom and Sarah Pritchard recently relocated due to a change in Tom's employment. The Pritchards were good moral people, and had attended church since childhood. One final aspect of the relocation was ahead of them: where to attend church. Like thousands of Americans, Tom and Sarah were church hunting.

New to the community, Tom and Sarah didn't know anything about the churches in town. Even coworkers confessed to either not attending church or not being satisfied with their houses of worship. Armed with a list they compiled from an Internet search, the couple visited one church after another.

This Sunday was like every other Sunday, a bright clear day that demonstrated God's goodness and beautiful creation. Grace Church was a few miles from Tom and Sarah's house, but the drive took only minutes. The church was identified by a marquee with a message of welcome and a reminder of service times. Directional signage on the parking lot and painted arrows on the pavement led the couple to a designated area for guests. A parking lot attendant greeted the couple with a friendly smile and wave. (Presentation 1) He gave the couple a brochure and coupons for free coffee and doughnuts inside. They parked the car and met another attendant who walked them into the church. (Presentation 2)

The attendant walked the couple to the main entrance and wished them a warm, "God bless you." Just then Tom noticed an elderly couple drive their car near the entrance to the building, and two attendants opened the driver and passenger doors and took their keys. Could this be valet service for senior adults?

Inside, Tom and Sarah were welcomed by greeters who smiled and shook their hands. (Presentation 3) One greeter asked if they were here to attend worship service or one of the classes. Another greeter escorted the Pritchards to the café to redeem the coffee coupons and introduced the couple to the barista behind the counter. (Presentation 4) As they entered the worship auditorium, an usher asked their seating preference and, in typical Grace Church form, led them to the area the couple selected. (Presentation 5)

Following a great service, (Presentation 6) the couple stopped at the restrooms to freshen up before leaving the church. The small but well-decorated restrooms were clean and well stocked with supplies and appropriate art.

A member of the church called Tom and Sarah that afternoon to thank them for their visit. (Presentation 7) A couple that lived near the Pritchards brought a basket of cookies later in the week. As the four talked, Tom and Sarah asked about the church and its ministries. (Presentation 8)

Tom and Sarah found their new church home.

Where is Grace Church? Grace Church is a composite of several churches I have visited as The Secret Church Shopper. (*www. secretchurchshopper.com*) A Secret Church Shopper helps pastors and churches evaluate their effectiveness.

The real message a church shares with its community begins in the parking lot, long before the minister delivers the Sunday morning sermon. From the restrooms to the greeters, everything guests encounter from the moment they arrive on the church property affects the worship experience.

Hospitality is one of the first things guests will notice about a church. The refrain, "We tried XYZ Church, but the people weren't very friendly," is uttered all too often. It is doubtful the people of XYZ Church were not friendly. It could be more correctly said they were not friendly enough.

A genuine concern for guests should be paramount in recruiting and training greeters and ushers. The art of hospitality and putting someone at ease is something guests appreciate. Since guests may be shy and even a little nervous about new people and surroundings, present with care.

The next thing guests notice is the cleanliness and maintenance of the facility. Whether it is a rented facility or a cathedral, how we maintain and care for the building God has provided speaks volumes.

The impressions (presentations) we make are not line items in the annual budget, but are an outcome of a spiritual attitude and discipline. We are quick to care for those in our congregation who are facing surgery or other emergencies of life. We need to focus attention on our guests to the point where we not only care for guests, we cultivate and minister to them in every way we communicate or present to them.

What do your guests experience from all the presentations they receive?

There is little doubt that the pastor's sermon plays a major role in a guest's first-time evaluation of a church. Visitors are looking for a connection in spiritual depth, style, doctrine, or vision. The style and authenticity of praise and worship also play a big role. It is important to remember, however, that other presentations made in and around the church—especially the first ones visitors encounter—are essential components of the whole visiting experience.

Each church member who makes a connection—from the parking attendant to the person who calls to follow up with the guest—can make a huge impact on a guest's decision to return. The warmth behind a smile, a welcoming comment, or clear directions can make all the difference for a visitor. The *Seven Steps to Effective Presentations* will help you think through the impact you are making. The steps will help you be prepared to make a real difference in this essential ministry.

If you are involved in any aspect of the first impressions ministry, greeting is certainly part of your role. Each member of the team has the opportunity to offer warmth, genuineness, friendliness, and even an encounter with God in the way he or she greets. Since greeting is such an important part of ministry, we will focus on the greeter position as we look at the presentation steps.

As a greeter, it is a good idea to work in teams of two so you can effectively handle the heavy traffic time that usually starts about fifteen minutes before the service begins. Teaming up to greet with a friend or spouse can be quite enjoyable. I have served as a greeter many times in our church, and I really enjoy working with my wife Tammy. We even have our two daughters help us from time to time. If we have something to hand out, the girls keep us supplied while we focus on greeting the people.

I am a very extroverted person, and I love to welcome people with a smile and a handshake. If you are not an extrovert, greeting may not come quite as naturally, but you can still do a great job. You will simply need to step out of your comfort zone a little and practice a lot.

As we look at the seven steps to see how they might apply to greeting, understand that presenting in the area of greeting is a little different. Greeters give many very short impromptu presentations over a short period of time. Preparation and forethought will help you become a more effective greeting presenter.

| Step 1: Clarify Objectives |

Your ultimate objective will likely be to make guests feel welcome and comfortable. So do all you can to help guests and regular attendees encounter the warmth, genuineness, friendliness, and encounter with God that they are seeking. Scripture shows that part of a person's encounter with God can be experienced when he encounters one of God's people. Second Corinthians 2:15 says "we are to God the aroma of Christ among those who are being saved and those who are perishing." You are representing Christ in every encounter you have, whether or not you are prepared to do so.

Other possible objectives include offering clear and pleasant directions, reducing the intimidation factor for visitors, or helping people make connections with others or essential ministries in your church. Reverend Harrison offered one more excellent piece of advice that fits with any objective. He said, "The last time I checked, handshakes and smiles were still free and legal." They are also effective. Give them out liberally.

Step 1 | EXAMPLE

A friend who directs the first impressions ministry of her church shared the story of Chet and Sharon, who connected quickly with their church as a result of the efforts of the first impressions team. Chet and Sharon and their eighteen-month-old daughter Alexis were visiting the church for the first time. They had been invited by an acquaintance who knew they were looking for a church that would be a good fit for them. Ruth was in the parking lot, and she knew her objective was to make visitors and regulars feel welcome and comfortable. When Chet, Sharon, and Alexis got out of their car, Ruth greeted them with a smile and a handshake and told them she was glad they came. Then she directed them into the building.

| Step 2: Define Your Audience |

As a greeter you often do not have much time to define your audience as people come in the door. Anyone who comes in will fit into one of three categories:

! People you know
! People you have seen before
! People who are there for the first time

When there are a lot of people coming in at the same time, you often do not even have time to make those distinctions in your head. You would like to greet those you know, and even those that you have seen before, differently than you greet the first-time guest. But what if you cannot remember who is new or don't have time to make a distinction?

We have found that it works well to simply say to everyone, "It's good to see you." It eliminates the guesswork and sends a clear welcoming message to each person you greet. If you have more time, you can ask a question or two such as, "How long have you been attending?" First time guests would then identify themselves as such by their response. Your team leader may have a different preference, so ask your leader what he or she wants you to say or accomplish.

You can quickly differentiate your audience by age. When a young child comes in while I am greeting, I often get on my knees and get on an eye-level with the child. Most of the time, parents are thrilled by the effort to make the child feel welcome, even if you are not putting all of your energy and effort into greeting them. A handshake for an elderly woman will likely be a little softer than a handshake with a young man. Whether you are greeting the young or old, meet them on their level.

STEP 2 | EXAMPLE

When Chet and Sharon got to the front door, Wanda greeted them with a big smile and a warm handshake. She knew she had not seen them before, so she introduced herself and told them how glad she was they were there. She spoke lovingly to Alexis and complimented her on her dress.

| STEP 3: GATHER CONTENT |

In this scenario, your primary content is going to be the training you received as a greeter. You could also gather information from others who have greeted before. Ask them for insights on comments and phrases that they use. When you attend an event as a visitor, pay special attention to how you are greeted.

Make sure you know how to direct guests to the different areas of the church. Find out where Sunday school classes for all ages are meeting. If you have a complicated campus, ask for or create a map that you can use. But please do not just hand out the maps. Open them and show people where to go. Draw the route in if it is complicated. Some larger churches have people serving as guides to take guests wherever they want to go. Know where to find your guides or identify the shortest route to the restrooms, information table, and other important areas in your church.

Keep in mind that no one wants to look like he is lost or confused. Guests do not want to park in the wrong spot or go into the wrong door. They don't want to wander down a hallway trying to find their way. Be as helpful as you can to make them feel comfortable. That may involve telling them that the service starts in twelve minutes. You may even show them where to stand in the transition while they are waiting for the first service to let out. Remember, you are the *ultimate host*, and you want to take care of your guests.

If you have been a greeter for a while, I bet you are thinking, "How in the world do I do all that during the rush when twenty or thirty families are coming in at the same time?" Think through rush times and bottlenecks with your team in advance. For example, make sure all hands are on deck at the peak time. Some churches have extra "floating" greeters available to help during crunch times. Floaters can also help when someone comes in with a special need (like prayer or encouragement), and it is hard for you to break away to handle it.

Before guests start arriving, find out whether there have been any changes in the normal schedule or routine. If construction is underway on some of the restrooms, find out where the backup restrooms are. If the Sunday school staff is shorthanded, find out if classes have been combined. Hopefully your team leader has a procedure in place to make sure the greeters are informed of any such changes, but it is always a good idea to ask ahead of time. Find out what the sermon is going to be about. Your preparation may make for a timely comment or a quick response to a visitor's question.

STEP 3 | EXAMPLE

Wanda told Chet and Sharon where the nursery was for Alexis, and she invited them to have coffee and bagels before the service at the church's coffee bar just outside the sanctuary doors. As they walked off, she told them again how nice it was to have them.

GATHERING CONTENT FOR OTHER SCENARIOS

If your job is to attend the information table, your content will be all of the informational pieces that you give out to guests and regular attendees. Look over the information in advance so you have a working knowledge of the ministries your church offers. Make sure you have enough brochures, flyers, information cards, or whatever else you hand out. Then go one step further and make sure you know where the additional boxes are in case you have a run on something. Find out who is responsible for having more printed if you start running low.

Ushers who hand out the bulletins or offering envelopes should know where the extra boxes are. Consider what you will do you if you run out of bulletins. Thinking through these scenarios ahead of time will save a lot of awkward moments and will help you make a better first impression.

If you attend the guest registration table and you have gifts or gift cards to hand to your guests, keep about a month's worth of gifts on hand. Since pencils and pens often have a habit of disappearing, keep plenty of extras nearby. Make sure you have basic knowledge of the ministries at your church. Guests may want to know what your church offers.

| STEP 4: MAXIMIZE PREPARATION |

I can't emphasize enough how important it is to plan ahead and have extra handouts ready. Whether you are handing out bulletins, maps, invitations, or roses on Mother's Day, be ready to quickly get more. It makes a poor impression if you have to leave your very busy post to go looking for more handouts.

Consider how weather affects your job and people as they arrive. Make sure walkways are clear of snow and ice. If it is raining outside, can you recruit more greeters to help walk in guests with umbrellas? Do you know where the coat and umbrella racks are? Think through as many scenarios as you can and be prepared for them so you can make an excellent first impression.

Since the actual interaction between the greeter and the audience is so short, you would likely not need to complete a 3-D Outline™. Just remember that your objective is to offer guests the warmth you would to any new family member, paying special attention to your body language and your role as ultimate host.

STEP 4 | EXAMPLE

Chet and Sharon were both surprised to see an usher standing near the front door with a wheelchair. They saw that he was watching people as they came from the parking lot up the long walk to the door, ready to help anyone in need of assistance. They were very impressed with the planning, thoughtfulness, and caring that went into such an act.

| STEP 5: OPEN WELL |

Research shows that roughly half of our communication (about fifty-five percent) takes place through our body language and about a third comes through tonality. That means that your words play a fairly small part. In this scenario, you will likely communicate with each person for less than a minute. Since your opening may be your only communication, it is vitally important that your body language complements your words and that your tone matches your body language. All three need to be saying, "We are really glad you are here!"

Body language includes your smile, your stance, and your gestures. It could also include actions like opening the door. Remember, your objective is to be the ultimate host and make your guests feel comfortable.

STEP 5 | EXAMPLE

Ron was the usher and greeter at the door of the sanctuary. Chet and Sharon could tell by his smile, handshake, and enthusiasm that Ron was genuinely glad they were there. Chet and Sharon had decided to take Alexis into the sanctuary with them on this visit. Ron introduced himself and talked with Alexis, coaxing a smile from her. Then he made sure they knew where the nursery was in case they changed their minds.

| STEP 6: ENGAGE YOUR AUDIENCE |

Keep in mind that your attention should be focused on your guests and others that are coming in. Your objective is to make *everyone* feel welcome. So this is not a time to spend visiting with friends. Do not spend so much time with one person or family that several more slip by unnoticed. Sometimes you can create a bad impression by simply not making a good impression. Overlooking someone unintentionally can create a lasting negative impression.

The type of greeting you give often depends on the relationship you have with the person. First-time guests, for example, are usually very intimidated by hugs. But if you have relationship with someone and know that he or she is comfortable with hugs, then go ahead and hug. I like to put my hand on the person's shoulder while I am shaking hands. It's more than a handshake but less than a hug. It works well for me, but you need to carefully think through any type of touching.

A great way to engage your guests is to call them by name. Make it a high priority to remember names. When you use their names the next time you see them, they will feel important, welcomed, and impressed! If time permits, ask questions to get the guests involved. Questions like, "Where are you from?" or "How long have you lived here?" can be answered with nice, short answers and do not start long and involved conversations. Be sure to follow up their responses with something like, "Great! We're glad you have chosen to be our guests today."

STEP 6 | EXAMPLE

Both Wanda and Ron had engaged Alexis by talking to her, but Ron took it a step further. He asked Chet and Sharon where they were from. When they responded that they lived in the city, he said, "Great. We're really glad you're here today." Then he gave them a bulletin and showed them inside the sanctuary, politely steering them close to the back in case they needed to take Alexis out.

Chet and Sharon were very impressed with the pastor, his sermon, and the entire service. After the service, they stopped by the guest registration table and turned in their guest card. Nonie introduced herself and gave them a gift card and some informational brochures about the church. She asked if they had any questions about the church and genuinely told them how glad she was that they were there. They were almost out the door when they heard Ron calling Chet's name. Thinking it must be someone who knew them, they turned and scanned the area. When they realized it was Ron, they were very impressed that he had remembered Chet's name. Ron invited them to come back the next Sunday, and even suggested that they get together for lunch sometime. Chet and Sharon left almost overwhelmed with the warmth, friendliness, and welcome they felt.

| STEP 7: CLOSE WITH ACTION |

There is so little actual communication time between the greeter and the guest that it is difficult to include an opening, closing, and something in between! You might show guests where the guest registration part of the bulletin is. If time permits, you may invite them to an upcoming special event. But the best "send-off" you can give them is to tell them again—with body language, tone, and words—that you are glad they came.

Many churches follow up with a phone call or home visit within forty-eight to seventy-two hours after the guest's first-time visit to the church. This is a very effective connection that tells the guest, "We really care about you and want you to come back." The person making the call or visit can answer questions about the ministry, find out a little about the background of the guest, and offer suggestions for connection. That often includes an invitation to a Bible study, a Sunday school class, or a special event.

STEP 7 | EXAMPLE

I guess you could say that Ron closed with action when he followed up with Chet and Sharon immediately after the service. In this case, Ron even included in the follow-up an invitation for a social visit. Chet and Sharon received a follow-up call from another member of the first impressions team within a few days of their first visit. Before too long, they joined the church and became involved in a small group. Today, they host a small group in their home and are part of the leadership team. They would likely tell you that they are still in that church today because they found four things during their first visit: warmth, genuineness, friendliness, and an encounter with God.

SCENARIO 9 VIP'S

! The heart and attitude of a church is displayed in the way its people connect with each other and with guests.

! Your first impressions team is the face of your ministry to visitors, and it serves as a representative of Christ to those who do not yet know him.

! Guests look for four things when they visit a church: warmth, genuineness, friendliness, and an encounter with God.

! Each church member who makes a connection—from the parking attendant to the person who calls to follow up with the guest—can make a huge impact on a guest's decision to return.

! Since your opening may be your only communication, it is vitally important that your body language complements your words and that your tone matches your body language. All three need to be saying, "We are really glad you are here!"

! The best "send-off" you can give your guests is to tell them again—with body language, tone, and words—that you are glad they came.

PREPARATION, PRESENTATION, AND POWER

> From him the whole body, joined and held together
> by every supporting ligament, grows and builds
> itself up in love, as each part does its work.

—EPHESIANS 4:16

Whatever your role in the church, I can tell you with certainty that it is vital to growing and building your local body to make it function as it should. The church is not a one-man show. As wonderful as pastors are, they cannot—and were never meant to—do the work alone. Ephesians 4:12, 13 clearly shows that they were given to the body, "*to prepare God's people for works of service*, so that the body of Christ may be built up until we all reach unity in the faith and in the knowledge of the Son of God and become mature, attaining to the whole measure of the fullness of Christ" (emphasis mine).

Whether you lead a small group, teach a Bible study or Sunday school class, train volunteers, interact with the media, volunteer for outreach events, or help host the service, you are part of a team that is working toward the highest calling. My goal with this book is to equip you with tools that will strengthen your efforts and help you to be an even more effective member of that team. Through *purpose-filled presentations* you can prepare and present with power that will change lives for eternity.

In Part 1 of the book, we talked about how the body of Christ is God's vehicle to deliver his message, and that he has empowered us with the gift of communication to accomplish that. I introduced the *Seven Steps to Effective Presentations* that will help you more powerfully deliver your message. I showed you how to have more confidence in your presentations by preparing well so you can make the unknowns known. I talked about how tempting it is to procrastinate, and how that can lead to nervousness and insufficient preparation. I hope you have a clear understanding of how the 3-D Outline™ can help you maximize your preparation by thinking through the *what*, *why*, and *how* of your presentation. It is a proven, simple process that can help you be more confident—even if you complete your 3-D Outline™ on a napkin.

We looked at the importance of engaging your audience and creating a winning situation for them. Audiences don't want to be talked at; they want to have a conversation. They feel more connected when they are involved and responding, so remember to keep your facilitation hat on a big portion of the time.

In Part 2 of the book, I talked about nine common scenarios for making presentations in and around the church. I put sharing your testimony first, because it often touches the other scenarios. Teaching a Sunday school class, leading a small group, leading a meeting, participating in an outreach event, and training others may involve sharing your testimony at some point, and you need to be ready to share when God opens a door. Your testimony is your story of God's work and transforming power in your life. You never know when he may use that story to bring light and hope to someone who does not know him or to encourage someone who does.

We applied the *Seven Steps to Effective Presentations* to each scenario chapter. I included the repetition and reinforcement to help you master a simple process that will help you prepare a powerful presentation each time you present.

Steps 1 and 2, "Clarify Objectives" and "Define Your Audience," often overlap and can even be switched in order if necessary. But it is essential to get clarity on your objectives and know your purpose behind what you want to accomplish at the very beginning. It is usually best to have no more than three or four objectives or to have one primary objective and a few secondary objectives.

As you are thinking through your objectives, remember to think about your audience. Remember that there may be several different types of audience members within the same audience. When you deliver in front of the church, for example, you need to think through who might be in your audience in addition to your usual church congregation. Your parents may be in the audience that day, or there may be visitors. People usually filter the message they hear through the context of the relationship they have with the presenter.

As we looked at step 3, "Gathering Content," we found that there are so many different sources available today. The Web certainly produces an unlimited amount of valuable information. Remember that learning from someone who has already done what you are doing can be very useful as well. I encourage you to carefully think through all of your resources, including those we have incorporated into Part 3 of this book. Just keep in mind that any content you use needs to be in alignment with your pastor, your church, your denomination, and most importantly, God's Word.

As you go through step 4, "Maximize Preparation," remember to pull from what you learned in Chapter 3 of the book. Pray and seek God's wisdom as you gather and sort through your information and build your 3-D Outline™ and agendas. Remember that not all procrastination is bad, but when it is linked to preparation it usually is. There are five steps that will help you be peaceful and calm as you present:

1. Seek God's direction
2. Be fully prepared
3. Be fully prepared in plenty of time
4. Ask God for his peace
5. Trust that God will be at work in both the presenting and receiving of his Word

As we looked at step 5, "Open Well," we looked at how you are making an impression long before you begin speaking. Opening well can even include guarding your reputation and good name in the church. People will begin making a judgment from invitations, e-mails, and initial conversations. They will decide if they want to hear more as the first words come out of your mouth. Remember to make an impact within those first few moments. Give your audience the purpose, process, and payoff right at the beginning. Let them know your objectives and where you are going with your presentation. Help them understand the value of your presentation.

In step 6, "Engage Your Audience," we discovered many great ideas for engagement. Think back to when you were in the audience in the scenario you are now presenting or preparing for. Were you engaged and connected the last time when you were in a meeting, training class, or Bible study? Can you remember a scenario in which you were fully engaged and very enthusiastic? Perhaps the presenter used an activity or a small group discussion to break up the session and keep you connected, or maybe he had you write notes or take a quiz. The presenter was probably facilitating at least some of the time.

Remember from our experience with the last step, "Close with Action," to think about what you want people to do as a result of hearing your message. You might challenge them to think differently about something or take some kind of specific action or to actually make a change in behavior. If you are teaching a children's class, you may remind kids to take something they have made or colored to their parents to explain what they learned. That way, your message will cascade to parents or siblings who may not even be part of your church.

These seven steps are not limited to the scenarios presented in this book. They can be used as a pattern for any purpose-filled presentation you make inside or outside of church. Think with me for a minute. What would happen if you made an effective presentation to your children about honoring God and his plan for their lives by being more diligent in their schoolwork? You could engage them in the process and actually have them tell you why they should be making good grades! Using the final step, "Close with Action," you could ask them to agree to put forth their very best effort in each subject.

Let's go one step further. What if your presentation included *any* choices they make in their youth—whether it is to live out their faith, choose the right friends, or stand up for what is right? Such presentations could make a powerful impact on your children, your family, your church, and your community. Just think what you could do if you adjusted this presentation to bring about God-honoring results with marriage, relationships with neighbors, or colleagues at work.

I believe the more diligently you apply the information in this book, the more effective your presentations will be. Pull it out and use it often. Make your own notes in the margin, underline the parts you want to remember, and turn down your favorite pages. Allow it to help you become more fully equipped to "do good works, which God has prepared in advance for us to do" (Ephesians 2:10). My prayer is that however you use the steps and ideas in this book, and in whatever scenario you use them, you will give an effective and powerful presentation, enjoy the process, and glorify God.

I have devoted Part 3 of this book to providing additional resources that will help you maximize your preparation for any presentation you make in your work for the kingdom of God. I have included many great books, Web sites, software programs, templates, activities, and other resources. I encourage you to become familiar with this section so you can better understand the wealth of information available to you. You may want to investigate adding to these and building your own library of resources to strengthen your effectiveness in making purpose-filled presentations.

And now I have a special request. If you have found this book to be helpful, please share it with other people. Tell your pastor, church educational director, other leaders, and many friends about it. I have truly invested decades on the subject of presentation effectiveness and so desire to have this book shared with thousands of Christians so they, like you, can be their best when sharing God's message. Finally, I pray for God to bless all of your (my readers') presentations!

PART

3

RESOURCES

Cat.	Resource & Description	Introduction-Equipped with Confidence	Chapter 1 Communicate (with excellence)	Chapter 2 Reduce Nervousness (and increase your confidence)	Chapter 3 Prepare (to maximize effectiveness)	Chapter 4 Engage (so everyone wins)	Scenario Chapter 1 Share Your Testimony	Scenario Chapter 2 Host a Worship Service	Scenario Chapter 3 Lead and Empower Small Groups	Scenario Chapter 4 Maximize Teaching Opportunities	Scenario Chapter 5 Train Others	Scenario Chapter 6 Lead a Great Meeting	Scenario Chapter 7 Interact with the Media	Scenario Chapter 8 Reach out to Others	Scenario Chapter 9 Create Great First Impressions	Audience
Books	*Forty Days of Purpose*, by Rick Warren									●						Adult Ministry
Books	*Care and Feeding of Volunteers*, by Barbara Bolton, Mike Bright, & Byron Cressy										●					Adult Training
Books	*Christian Minister's Manual* (available through standardpub.com)										●					Adult Training
Books	*Inspire Any Audience*, by Tony Jeary		●													Adult Training
Books	*Training for Service Leader's Guide*, by Orrin Root										●					Adult Training
Books	*Training for Service Student Book*, by Orrin Root										●					Adult Training
Books	*Presenting with Style*, by Robert Rohm and Tony Jeary		●													Advanced Presenters
Books	*Treat 'Em Right!: Tasty Ideas for Encouraging Volunteers*, by Susan Cutshall										●					Children's Ministry
Books	*200+ Activities for Children's Ministry*, by Susan Lingo									●						Children's Ministry
Books	*30 New Testament Interactive Stories for Young Children*, by Steven James									●						Children's Ministry
Books	*30 New Testament QuickSkits for Kids*, by Steven James									●						Children's Ministry
Books	*30 Old Testament Interactive Stories for Young Children*, by Steven James									●						Children's Ministry
Books	*Bible Story QuickSkits for 2 Kids*, by Steven James									●						Children's Ministry

Cat.	Resource & Description	Introduction-Equipped with Confidence	Chapter 1 Communicate (with excellence)	Chapter 2 Reduce Nervousness (and increase your confidence)	Chapter 3 Prepare (to maximize effectiveness)	Chapter 4 Engage (so everyone wins)	Scenario Chapter 1 Share Your Testimony	Scenario Chapter 2 Host a Worship Service	Scenario Chapter 3 Lead and Empower Small Groups	Scenario Chapter 4 Maximize Teaching Opportunities	Scenario Chapter 5 Train Others	Scenario Chapter 6 Lead a Great Meeting	Scenario Chapter 7 Interact with the Media	Scenario Chapter 8 Reach out to Others	Scenario Chapter 9 Create Great First Impressions	Audience
Books	*Crazy & Creative Bible Stories for Preteens*, by Steven James									•						Children's Ministry
Books	*Do-It-Yourself Children's Ministry Handbook* (available through standardpub.com)										•					Children's Ministry
Books	*Energizing Children's Ministry in the Smaller Church*, by Rick Chromey										•					Children's Ministry
Books	*Leading Preteens: A Growing Ministry Guide*, by Patrick Snow										•					Children's Ministry
Books	*More 200+ Activities for Children's Ministry*, by Susan Lingo									•						Children's Ministry
Books	*Sharable Parables*, by Steven James									•						Children's Ministry
Books	*Sharable Parables: Creative Storytelling Ideas* for Ages 3-12, by Steven James									•						Children's Ministry
Books	*Teaching with Heart*, by Jody Capehart										•					Children's Ministry
Books	*The Creative Storytelling Guide for Children's Ministry*, by Steven James									•						Children's Ministry
Books	*You-Can-Do-It Family Ministry Events*, by Susan Martins Miller									•						Children's Ministry
Books	*Life Is a Series of Presentations*, by Tony Jeary	•														General
Books	*Maximize Your Media Presentations: Great Tips for Dealing with the Media*, by Kim Dower and Tony Jeary												•			Media Spokespersons
Books	*Meeting Magic*, by Tony Jeary and George Lowe											•				Meeting Leaders

Cat.	Resource & Description	Introduction-Equipped with Confidence	Chapter 1 Communicate (with excellence)	Chapter 2 Reduce Nervousness (and increase your confidence)	Chapter 3 Prepare (to maximize effectiveness)	Chapter 4 Engage (so everyone wins)	Scenario Chapter 1 Share Your Testimony	Scenario Chapter 2 Host a Worship Service	Scenario Chapter 3 Lead and Empower Small Groups	Scenario Chapter 4 Maximize Teaching Opportunities	Scenario Chapter 5 Train Others	Scenario Chapter 6 Lead a Great Meeting	Scenario Chapter 7 Interact with the Media	Scenario Chapter 8 Reach out to Others	Scenario Chapter 9 Create Great First Impressions	Audience
Books	*We've Got to Stop Meeting Like This*, by George Lowe and Tony Jeary											●				Meeting Leaders
Books	*Beyond Your Backyard*, by Tom Ellsworth													●		Outreach Ministry
Books	*Go!* by Arron Chambers													●		Outreach Ministry
Books	*Just Walk Across the Room*, by Bill Hybels													●		Outreach Ministry
Books	*Life on Loan*, by Rick Rusaw													●		Outreach Ministry
Books	*Outflow*, by Steve Sjogren													●		Outreach Ministry
Books	*Tony Evans Speaks Out on Being Single and Satisfied*, by Tony Evans										●					Singles
Books	*Living a Life of Balance: Women of Faith Study Guide Series*								●							Women
Books	*A Time to Speak*, compiled by Henrietta Gambill							●								Worship Ministry
Books	*Holiday Program Books* (available through standardpub.com)							●								Worship Ministry
Books	*In the Breaking of Bread*, by J. Lee Magness							●								Worship Ministry
Books	*The Longest Table*, by J. Lee Magness							●								Worship Ministry
Books	*Middle School Ministry Made Simple*, by Kurt Johnston										●					Adult Ministry
Curriculum	*Box Office Bible Studies: Isaiah*, by Jim Eichenberger (available through standardpub.com)								●	●						Adult Ministry

Cat.	Resource & Description	Introduction-Equipped with Confidence	Chapter 1 Communicate (with excellence)	Chapter 2 Reduce Nervousness (and increase your confidence)	Chapter 3 Prepare (to maximize effectiveness)	Chapter 4 Engage (so everyone wins)	Scenario Chapter 1 Share Your Testimony	Scenario Chapter 2 Host a Worship Service	Scenario Chapter 3 Lead and Empower Small Groups	Scenario Chapter 4 Maximize Teaching Opportunities	Scenario Chapter 5 Train Others	Scenario Chapter 6 Lead a Great Meeting	Scenario Chapter 7 Interact with the Media	Scenario Chapter 8 Reach out to Others	Scenario Chapter 9 Create Great First Impressions	Audience
Curriculum	*Box Office Bible Studies: Acts,* by Jim Eichenberger (available through standardpub.com)								•	•						Adult Ministry
Curriculum	*Box Office Bible Studies: Leadership,* by Jim Eichenberger (available through standardpub.com)								•	•						Adult Ministry
Curriculum	*Crash Course on Jesus* (available through standardpub.com)								•	•						Adult Ministry
Curriculum	*Crash Course on Psalms* (available through standardpub.com)								•	•						Adult Ministry
Curriculum	*Crash Course on Revelation* (available through standardpub.com)								•	•						Adult Ministry
Curriculum	*Crash Course on the New Testament* (available through standardpub.com)								•	•						Adult Ministry
Curriculum	*Crash Course on the Old Testament* (available through standardpub.com)								•	•						Adult Ministry
Curriculum	Faith Café Curriculum (available through standardpub.com/faithcafe)								•	•						Adult Ministry
Curriculum	On Demand Bible Studies: Good from Evil, by Bob Russell								•	•						Adult Ministry
Curriculum	On Demand Bible Studies: Nobody's Perfect, by Bob Russell								•	•						Adult Ministry
Curriculum	On Demand Bible Studies: Promises, Promises, by Bob Russell								•	•						Adult Ministry

Cat.	Resource & Description	Introduction-Equipped with Confidence	Chapter 1 Communicate (with excellence)	Chapter 2 Reduce Nervousness (and increase your confidence)	Chapter 3 Prepare (to maximize effectiveness)	Chapter 4 Engage (so everyone wins)	Scenario Chapter 1 Share Your Testimony	Scenario Chapter 2 Host a Worship Service	Scenario Chapter 3 Lead and Empower Small Groups	Scenario Chapter 4 Maximize Teaching Opportunities	Scenario Chapter 5 Train Others	Scenario Chapter 6 Lead a Great Meeting	Scenario Chapter 7 Interact with the Media	Scenario Chapter 8 Reach out to Others	Scenario Chapter 9 Create Great First Impressions	Audience
Curriculum	On Demand Bible Studies: Risky Creation, by Bob Russell								●	●						Adult Ministry
Curriculum	*Tuning Into God: George Strait* (available through standardpub.com)								●	●						Adult Ministry
Curriculum	*Tuning Into God: Rolling Stones* (available through standardpub.com)								●	●						Adult Ministry
Curriculum.	*Tuning Into God: The Beatles* (available through standardpub.com)								●	●						Adult Ministry
Curriculum	*Tuning Into God: The Eagles* (available through standardpub.com)								●	●						Adult Ministry
Curriculum	The Standard Lesson Quarterly (available through standardpub.com)								●	●						Adult Ministry
Curriculum	"Object Talks" Series, by Susan Lingo (available through standardpub.com)									●						Children's Ministry
Curriculum	Around the World CAMP, by Tracy Carpenter									●						Children's Ministry
Curriculum	CAMP Curriculum, by Tracy Carpenter									●						Children's Ministry
Curriculum	Country Fair CAMP, by Tracy Carpenter									●						Children's Ministry
Curriculum	God Rocks! BibleToons curriculum (available through standardpub.com)									●						Children's Ministry
Curriculum	Kid's Choice CAMP, by Tracy Carpenter									●						Children's Ministry
Curriculum	Route 52 Curriculum (available through standardpub.com)									●						Children's Ministry
Curriculum	SuperStart! A Preteen Curriculum! (available at www.superstartpreteen.com)									●						Children's Ministry

Cat.	Resource & Description	Introduction-Equipped with Confidence	Chapter 1 Communicate (with excellence)	Chapter 2 Reduce Nervousness (and increase your confidence)	Chapter 3 Prepare (to maximize effectiveness)	Chapter 4 Engage (so everyone wins)	Scenario Chapter 1 Share Your Testimony	Scenario Chapter 2 Host a Worship Service	Scenario Chapter 3 Lead and Empower Small Groups	Scenario Chapter 4 Maximize Teaching Opportunities	Scenario Chapter 5 Train Others	Scenario Chapter 6 Lead a Great Meeting	Scenario Chapter 7 Interact with the Media	Scenario Chapter 8 Reach out to Others	Scenario Chapter 9 Create Great First Impressions	Audience
Curriculum	Discovering the Jesus Answers book & guide (available through standardpub.com)								•	•						Youth Ministry
Curriculum	Discuss It: 50 Quizzes, Challenges, and Deep Questions (available through standardpub.com)									•						Youth Ministry
Curriculum	Discuss It: 50 Role Plays and Case Studies (available through standardpub.com)									•						Youth Ministry
Curriculum	Encounter Digital Bible Lessons (available through standardpub.com)									•						Youth Ministry
Curriculum	Finding the Jesus Experience book & guide (available through standardpub.com)								•	•						Youth Ministry
Curriculum	Jesus No Equal Journal, by Barry St. Clair								•	•						Youth Ministry
Curriculum	Jesus No Equal, by Barry St. Clair								•	•						Youth Ministry
Curriculum	Knowing the Real Jesus book & guide (available through standardpub.com)								•	•						Youth Ministry
Curriculum	Meeting the Jesus Challenge book & guide (available through standardpub.com)								•	•						Youth Ministry
Curriculum	On the Altar: Dedicate, by Garth Heckman									•						Youth Ministry
Curriculum	On the Altar: Surrender, by Garth Heckman									•						Youth Ministry
Curriculum	Skits for Student Ministry: ILLUSTRATE Bible Truths from Another Angle (available through standardpub.com)									•						Youth Ministry

Cat.	Resource & Description	Introduction—Equipped with Confidence	Chapter 1 Communicate (with excellence)	Chapter 2 Reduce Nervousness (and increase your confidence)	Chapter 3 Prepare (to maximize effectiveness)	Chapter 4 Engage (so everyone wins)	Scenario Chapter 1 Share Your Testimony	Scenario Chapter 2 Host a Worship Service	Scenario Chapter 3 Lead and Empower Small Groups	Scenario Chapter 4 Maximize Teaching Opportunities	Scenario Chapter 5 Train Others	Scenario Chapter 6 Lead a Great Meeting	Scenario Chapter 7 Interact with the Media	Scenario Chapter 8 Reach out to Others	Scenario Chapter 9 Create Great First Impressions	Audience
Curriculum	Skits for Student Ministry: INTRODUCE Bible Topics from Another Angle (available through standardpub.com)									•						Youth Ministry
Curriculum	Skits for Student Ministry: RETELL Bible Narratives from Another Angle (available through standardpub.com)									•						Youth Ministry
Curriculum	The Late Great Ape Debate book and discussion guide, by Bayard Taylor								•	•						Youth Ministry
Curriculum	The Revelation Epic: Chapters 5-22, by David Olshine								•	•						Youth Ministry
Curriculum	The Revelation Letters: Chapters 1-4, by David Olshine								•	•						Youth Ministry
Curriculum	True to Life: 40 Instant Studies: Old Testament (available through standardpub.com)									•						Youth Ministry
Curriculum	True to Life: 40 Instant Studies—Bible Truths (available through standardpub.com)									•						Youth Ministry
Curriculum	True to Life: 40 Instant Studies—New Testament (available through standardpub.com)									•						Youth Ministry
Electronic Tools	3-D Outline™ Software (access at www.mrpresentation.com)		•	•	•		•	•	•	•	•		•			General
Electronic Tools	Presentation Mastery Library, by Tony Jeary (access at www.mrpresentation.com)		•	•	•	•										General
Openers	Excerpts from Icebreakers, modified for Christian setting (available at purposefilledpresentations.com)					•										General

Cat.	Resource & Description	Introduction-Equipped with Confidence	Chapter 1 Communicate (with excellence)	Chapter 2 Reduce Nervousness (and increase your confidence)	Chapter 3 Prepare (to maximize effectiveness)	Chapter 4 Engage (so everyone wins)	Scenario Chapter 1 Share Your Testimony	Scenario Chapter 2 Host a Worship Service	Scenario Chapter 3 Lead and Empower Small Groups	Scenario Chapter 4 Maximize Teaching Opportunities	Scenario Chapter 5 Train Others	Scenario Chapter 6 Lead a Great Meeting	Scenario Chapter 7 Interact with the Media	Scenario Chapter 8 Reach out to Others	Scenario Chapter 9 Create Great First Impressions	Audience
Openers	Icebreakers by Tony Jeary (access at mrpresentation.com)									•						General
Reference Books	Standard Bible Atlas (available through standardpub.com)									•						Adult Ministry
Reference Books	Standard Bible Dictionary (available through standardpub.com)									•						Adult Ministry
Reference Books	Standard Reference Library: New Testament Volume One (available through standardpub.com)									•						Adult Ministry
Reference Books	Standard Reference Library: New Testament Volume Two (available through standardpub.com)									•						Adult Ministry
Reference Books	Standard Reference Library: Old Testament Volume One (available through standardpub.com)									•						Adult Ministry
Reference Books	Standard Reference Library: Old Testament Volume Two (available through standardpub.com)									•						Adult Ministry
Reference Books	Standard Reference Library: Old Testament Volume Three (available through standardpub.com)									•						Adult Ministry
Stories & Anecdotes	*Speaking Spice* by Tony Jeary and John Davis (access at mrpresentation.com)					•										General
Templates	3-D Outline™ (Available at tonyjeary.com)		•	•	•		•	•	•	•	•	•				Faster Preparation
Templates	DISC Model (See p. 236)		•													General

Cat.	Resource & Description	Introduction-Equipped with Confidence	Chapter 1 Communicate (with excellence)	Chapter 2 Reduce Nervousness (and increase your confidence)	Chapter 3 Prepare (to maximize effectiveness)	Chapter 4 Engage (so everyone wins)	Scenario Chapter 1 Share Your Testimony	Scenario Chapter 2 Host a Worship Service	Scenario Chapter 3 Lead and Empower Small Groups	Scenario Chapter 4 Maximize Teaching Opportunities	Scenario Chapter 5 Train Others	Scenario Chapter 6 Lead a Great Meeting	Scenario Chapter 7 Interact with the Media	Scenario Chapter 8 Reach out to Others	Scenario Chapter 9 Create Great First Impressions	Audience
Templates	Small Group Covenant (See p. 237)							•								Small Groups
Video	*Inspire Any Audience,* by Tony Jeary										•					Adult Training
Web sites	www.Rbpadultministries.org									•						Adult Ministry
Web sites	www.teachsundayschool.com									•						Adult Ministry
Web sites	www.about.com (Search: Sunday School)									•						Children's Ministry
Web sites	www.christiancrafters.com									•						Children's Ministry
Web sites	www.ehow.com (Search: Sunday School)									•						Children's Ministry
Web sites	www.kidssundayschool.com									•						Children's Ministry
Web sites	www.ministrytochildren.com									•						Children's Ministry
Web sites	www.ministry-to-children.com									•						Children's Ministry
Web sites	www.psscentral.com (Preschool Sunday School Central)									•						Children's Ministry
Web sites	www.vacationbibleschool.com									•						Children's Ministry
Web sites	www.spiritualcompassmarketing.com												•			Church Marketers
Web sites	www.standardpub.com									•						Church Resources
Web sites	www.Artofeloquence.com		•													General
Web sites	www.jokes.christiansunite.com				•											General
Web sites	www.mrpresentation.com	•	•	•	•						•	•	•		•	General
Web sites	www.ssconnection.net										•					General
Web sites	www.tonyjeary.com		•													General
Web sites	http://www.ncsl.org												•			Media Spokespersons
Web sites	http://www.tml.org												•			Media Spokespersons

Cat.	Resource & Description	Introduction-Equipped with Confidence	Chapter 1 Communicate (with excellence)	Chapter 2 Reduce Nervousness (and increase your confidence)	Chapter 3 Prepare (to maximize effectiveness)	Chapter 4 Engage (so everyone wins)	Scenario Chapter 1 Share Your Testimony	Scenario Chapter 2 Host a Worship Service	Scenario Chapter 3 Lead and Empower Small Groups	Scenario Chapter 4 Maximize Teaching Opportunities	Scenario Chapter 5 Train Others	Scenario Chapter 6 Lead a Great Meeting	Scenario Chapter 7 Interact with the Media	Scenario Chapter 8 Reach out to Others	Scenario Chapter 9 Create Great First Impressions	Audience
Web sites	www.saddleback.com													●		Outreach Ministry
Web sites	www.secretchurchshopper.com														●	Outreach Ministry
Web sites	www.servantevangelism.com													●		Outreach Ministry
Web sites	http://www.zyworld.com/PURENHART2/encouragingwordsforchristiansingles.htm								●							Singles
Web sites	www.about.com (Search: Youth Ministry)									●						Youth Ministry
Web sites	www.Rbpstudentministries.org									●						Youth Ministry
Web sites	www.simplyyouthministry.com									●						Youth Ministry
Web sites	www.teenmailbiblestudy.org (Free teen Bible study daily)									●						Youth Ministry
Workshop	Inspire Any Audience, by Tony Jeary										●					Adult Training
Workshop	Training Other People to Train, Tony Jeary										●					Adult Training
Workshop	Winning Seminars, by Tony Jeary (access at mrpresentation.com)		●	●	●	●										General

Outgoing-Task-Oriented | Outgoing-People-Oriented

Dominant

Direct

Demanding

Decisive

Determined

Doer

Inspiring

Influencing

Impressionable

Interested in People

Interactive

Impressive

Percentage of
population:
10-15%

Percentage of
population:
25-30%

Percentage of
population:
20-25%

Percentage of
population:
30-35%

D I
C S

Cautious

Calculating

Competent

Conscientious

Contemplative

Careful

Supportive

Stable

Steady

Sweet

Status Quo

Shy

Reserved-Task-Oriented | Reserved-People-Oriented

| SMALL GROUP COVENANT |

Our group covenant will guide us in our values with one another and bring harmony to our collective expectations and goals.

GROUP PURPOSE

[As a group, define your purpose for being together.]

GROUP VALUES

RELATIONSHIPS: While discussion of the curriculum, sharing, and prayer are key elements in a community group, a driving value of this group will be the building of relationships.

AUTHENTICITY: A community group should encourage openness and transparency within the group. We will create an environment where everyone feels free to be themselves.

SCRIPTURE: While everyone's thoughts and opinions are valued and encouraged, we will ultimately rely on the truth of Scripture as our final authority.

CONFIDENTIALITY: For authenticity to occur, we will commit and trust that issues of a personal nature that are discussed in the group are safe and will not be shared outside the group.

RESPECT: Group members should never say anything that will embarrass or dishonor someone else in the group.

AVAILABILITY: A primary responsibility of a community is to prioritize the relationships in the group. We will make the group a priority and will make ourselves available to each other's needs.

CONFLICT: We will seek to reconcile differences, hurts, and offenses with each other quickly, directly, prayerfully, and lovingly.

GROWTH AND MULTIPLICATION: Healthy communities grow as they extend invitations to their friends. At a designated date, we will seek to multiply the group's influence by starting one or more new groups.

GROUP LOGISTICS

Day and time of group meeting:

We will meet: Every week   Every other week

Our plan to invite new people to the group will be:

How will we handle childcare?

How will we handle snacks?

Who will handle these roles within the group?

Facilitating 1. _____ 2. _____

Hosting 1. _____ 2. _____

Organizing the prayer sheet: _____

Group communication: _____

Fellowship organizer: _____

Service project organizer: _____

GROUP GOALS

1.

2.

3.

Signed _____ Date _____

See Christ Church—Oak Brook Web site, http://my.cc-ob.org/Content/10127/72090.pdf

ABOUT THE AUTHOR

Tony Jeary—Mr. Presentation™—is known in the business world as a "Coach to the World's Top CEOs." Tony has seen ups and downs in his life—he made and lost millions before his 30th birthday. Then in the mid 80s, he began focusing on the subject of presentation effectiveness and, for the last twenty-five years, has been advising top performers from all over the globe on how to best present with impact. His clients include presidents of Wal-Mart, Sam's Club, American Airlines, and New York Life.

Tony has authored dozens of books—fourteen specifically on the subject of presentations. His platform has grown by the height of his clients who fly in from around the world to his private presentation studio in the Dallas area, where he lives with his beautiful wife and two daughters.

Tony grew up in a loving Christian home, attended Christian schools, and was raised by an entrepreneurial family. Having been blessed with an extensive platform, he prayerfully envisions taking his presentation expertise and sharing it broadly in the Christian arena. This book is the foundation for that vision.

Tony welcomes your communication and ideas on how to help millions of people with this book. He can be reached at www.tonyjeary.com or directly at info@tonyjeary.com. He encourages you to take advantage of many great free resources at www.purposefilledpresentations.com and requests that you will share this book with your friends as a gift or recommendation.

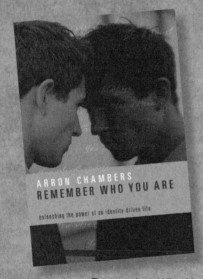